GOOD HOUSEKEEPING
Home Made Wine
& Beer

GOOD HOUSEKEEPING
Home Made Wine
& Beer

S W Andrews

EBURY PRESS
LONDON

First published 1974 by
Ebury Press
Chestergate House, Vauxhall Bridge Road,
London SW1V 1HF

© The National Magazine Co. Ltd 1974

ISBN 0 85223 045 1

Edited by Gill Edden
Drawings by Chris Evans

Printed in Great Britain by
Ebenezer Baylis & Son Ltd, The Trinity Press,
Worcester, and London
and bound by Mansell (Bookbinders) Ltd
Witham, Essex

Contents

Colour Plates

Introduction and Glossary

This chapter is written especially for beginners. The wine making process is explained in simple terms so that later, when reading a whole chapter devoted to a single stage, you will see clearly where it fits into the complete process. At the end of this chapter, in the glossary, the meanings of various technical terms used throughout the book are explained.

The process

Wine is made by fermenting fruit juice or an extraction from vegetables, herbs, flowers or grain. Water and sugar are added, together with other ingredients such as tannin and acid which will help give a balanced wine. The mixture of these ingredients is called a *must* (pages 25–51). Fermentation is caused by *yeast* (page 35). The natural yeasts found in all fruits and vegetables would cause an uncontrolled fermentation which could spoil the must very quickly and the latter is therefore sterilised and a selected wine yeast is introduced – one that has been specifically cultured for wine making. Using a selected yeast like this, it is possible to control fermentation and produce a good, balanced wine.

When starting to make a batch of wine, first sterilise all equipment with a sulphite solution (page 24). Next prepare the must according to your chosen recipe and sterilise that too; vegetables and dried fruits are sterilised by boiling in water, flower petals and herbs by pouring boiling water over them; all fresh fruit juice or pulp is sterilised with a sulphite solution (page 34). Sterilisation of equipment and ingredients ensures that there can be no contamination by bacteria and other micro organisms which might upset the wine.

The next stage is to balance the *acid* and *tannin* content of the must, usually with small quantities of citric or tartaric acid (page 47) and grape tannin (page 50). Then add a *yeast nutrient* (page 39) to assist yeast growth. Yeast takes a little time to become active even when presented with ideal conditions, and you must therefore start the yeast culture into activity several days before it will be required (page 40). After adding the active culture, fit an *airlock* (page 17) to the fermentation vessel and place the vessel somewhere where the temperature will remain constant at about 70°F (21°C) for up to a week, for the *primary fermentation* (page 53).

Next press the pulp and strain the juice into a storage jar, re-fit the airlock and leave at the slightly lower temperature of about 65°F (18°C) for the *secondary fermentation* (page 53). When the secondary fermentation is finished the young wine will probably be dry and can be *racked* (transferred into a fresh jar, leaving behind the *lees*) for storage (page 65). If a sweet wine is required, more sugar has to be added, which will probably prolong fermentation (page 56).

After racking, store the wine in a cool place to clear and *stabilise*. To help this process along, rack the wine once or twice more at 2-monthly intervals then, when it is clear and stable, bottle it (page 68). Further storage in bottle will bring the wine to the point where it is ready to be drunk.

Using a recipe

Having discussed the process, let us now make a gallon of orange wine. Oranges are available most of the year, but use only first class fruit as inferior fruit will give a wine that will lack quality. You should get 6 bottles of wine to the gallon.

Ingredients
all purpose yeast
15 sweet oranges
1 gal. (4.5 l.) water, approx.
1 tsp. pectolase
1 Campden tablet
3 lb. (1.4 kg.) white granulated sugar
2 level tsps. citric acid
1 level tsp. yeast nutrient

Equipment
Polythene bucket
2 x 1-gal. storage jars
1-litre bottle
Small saucepan
Wooden spoon
Medium-sized funnel
Nylon strainer
3 ft. rubber tubing with $\frac{1}{4}$-in. bore,
Measuring jug
Lemon squeezer
Airlock
1 jar cork, bored for airlock
Cotton wool
10-fl. oz. bottle
6 wine bottles, punted
6 bottle corks
1 jar cork, unbored

The yeast starter
To 4 fl. oz. fresh orange juice add $\frac{1}{2}$ oz. sugar. Sterilise this by boiling it for 5 minutes, cool it and pour into a 10-fl. oz. bottle which has been well washed and sterilised with sulphite solution B (page 24) and rinsed with boiled water. Plug the opening with cotton wool. When the juice has cooled to 70°F (21°C) add the yeast. Replace the cotton wool and stand the bottle in a warm place at 70°F to reactivate the yeast. After 3 days prepare the ingredients for the must.

Preparation of ingredients
Cut the oranges in half and extract the juice, using a lemon squeezer. Strain the juice through the nylon sieve; discard the pulp and pips. Measure the juice and make it up to 6 pt. with cold water. Pour this into the polythene bucket and add the pectolase. Now add the crushed Campden tablet, cover the bucket with a piece of polythene sheeting tied into position, leave at room temperature for 24 hours.

Preparation of the must
Add 3 lb. sugar to 2 pt. of water and bring to the boil. Add citric acid and yeast nutrient. Cool to 80°F (27°C) and then add to the orange

juice. Now incorporate the active yeast culture and stir the must with a wooden spoon. Pour the must into a gallon jar until it is seven-eighths full, then fit the airlock and stand the jar in a warm place at 70°F (21°C). Pour the remainder of the must into the litre bottle, plug the mouth firmly with a plug of cotton wool and stand it by the side of the large jar.

If you like a sweet wine with more orange flavour, add some rind to the must in the litre bottle. Pare the rind from 3 oranges VERY thinly, making sure that you do not include any of the pith or the wine will be bitter. Add this peel to the must in the litre bottle. (Strain the liquid off the peel before topping up the gallon jar.)

The fermentation

Do not be surprised if you see no action for 24–36 hours. During this period the yeasts are multiplying in readiness for fermentation. When the wine starts to ferment gas bubbles will be formed, these will rise to the surface, and collect there as froth. When this vigorous action has subsided, about a week later, you can top up the gallon jar with the wine from the litre bottle. Fill the jar to within 1 in. of the bottom of the cork. Stand the jar in a temperature of 65°F (18°C) until all bubbling has ceased.

Taste the wine; it will probably taste dry. If you want a dry wine it can be racked. If you want a sweet wine it will have to be fed with more sugar, as follows. As the wine nears the end of fermentation, and begins to taste dry, dissolve 4 oz. sugar in 2 fl. oz. boiling water and cool. Syphon some of the wine from the jar, add the sugar syrup and top up with some of the syphoned wine, replace the airlock and ferment on. If the wine again goes dry, repeat the process, until fermentation ceases. Sweeten the wine to taste with sugar syrup, rack into a clean jar, and proceed as for a dry wine.

Racking

Transfer the wine from the fermentation jar to another clean and sterile jar, leaving behind the lees. This is done by using a syphon. The rubber tubing is used for this purpose; one end is placed in the wine, the other end is sucked by mouth to start the syphon going and the wine is then run into the clean jar.

When all the wine has been transferred, top it up with boiled cold water to within $\frac{1}{4}$ in. of the cork and stand it in a cold place to clear.

Never store wine with an air space of more than $\frac{1}{4}$ in. otherwise it may develop disorders. The wine should be racked at least twice more at 2-monthly intervals. If after 6 months the wine is clear and shows no sign of fermentation it can be bottled. To make sure that fermentation has ceased, taste it; if it gives a prickling sensation on the tongue, delay bottling until this has completely disappeared.

Clarification
A wine that is still cloudy after 6 months can be fined with proprietary fining material obtained from equipment suppliers. Use as directed on the packet.

Bottling
Add half a crushed Campden tablet to the wine before bottling.

Punted wine bottles should be used. Clean the bottles by washing them well, and rinsing them with sulphite solution; finally the bottles should be rinsed with cold boiled water. Syphon the wine into the bottles using the rubber tubing. Fill them to within $\frac{1}{2}$ in. of the bottom of the cork. Soak straight-sided corks overnight in sulphite solution before use, wipe the corks dry with a clean cloth and drive them home with a mallet.

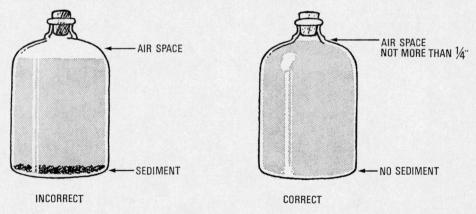

Never store wine with an airspace in the container of more than $\frac{1}{4}$ in.

Cellaring
Store the bottles on their sides so the wine is in contact with the cork, in a cool, dark place, free from vibration. Orange wine can be drunk young but will improve with keeping.

GLOSSARY

Acetified wine Wine which has been contaminated by vinegar bacteria.

Acid Acid gives a wine bite, a wine which lacks acid is said to be flabby, or flat. The three main acids found in wine are tartaric, citric and malic. Succinic acid is also present in small amounts.

Acid titration A method of determining the acid content of must or wine. The acid is neutralised by an alkaline solution of known strength, the amount of alkaline solution used is measured and this indicates the amount of acid present.

Agar Gelatinous substance used as a solidifying agent in culture media for bacteria, etc.

Airlock A piece of equipment which seals the mouth of a vessel during fermentation.

Alcohol Alcohol is produced by yeast action on sugar during fermentation. The main alcohol in wine is ethyl; wine also contains traces of some higher alcohols including amyl, butyl and propyl.

Aperitif A drink which is taken before a meal to stimulate the appetite and the flow of gastric juices.

Autolysis The process by which cells which have completed their life cycle are broken down by their own intra-cellular enzymes.

Blending The mixing of two or more wines together. Wines which are slightly unbalanced are often improved by judicious blending. Quality wines are never blended with inferior wines; the only result would be to introduce mediocrity to the quality wine.

Body The feel of wine in the mouth. It is related to the wine extract and alcohol content.

Bouquet The smell, or 'nose' of the wine.

Carbon dioxide The gas which is produced during fermentation.

Casks Wooden barrels used for the storage of wine.

Clarification Clearing a wine by removing the hazes which are caused by yeast cells, starch, pulp particles etc.

Disgorgement   A method of collecting sediment on the cork. The neck of the bottle is frozen, the cork removed and the pressure in the bottle expels the plug of sediment. The bottle is then topped up and re-corked.

Enzyme   A chemical compound without life. It has the power to change a substance without itself being changed.

Ester   Any class of organic compound formed by the interaction of an acid and an alcohol.

Feeding   A method of making a wine with a high alcohol content by adding small quantities of sugar syrup to a fermenting wine as it nears dryness.

Fermentation   Conversion of a sugary juice by yeasts into wine.

Filtration   Passing a wine through a filter to remove a haze, or to 'polish' it.

Flowers of wine   A wine disease caused by a film yeast. The surface of the wine becomes covered by a greyish white film.

Fortification   The addition of alcohol to wine. Sherry, port and Madeira are examples of fortified wines.

Gravity   The sugar content of a wine when measured by a hydrometer; another word for volume weight.

Hydrometer   An instrument used to measure the sugar content of a liquid.

Lees   The sediment on the bottom of a storage container.

Malo-lactic fermentation   A chemical reaction caused by a lactic acid bacteria. This helps to mellow the wine as it changes the hard malic acid to the softer lactic acid, producing a small amount of carbon dioxide as a by-product.

Mash   To mix malt with hot water.

Maturing   Storing wine to mellow it and to reduce harshness.

Must   The mixture of ingredients from which wine is to be made.

Pearson square   A formula used to calculate the required amount of sugar when adjusting the sugar content of a must.

Pétillant   The word used to describe wine which sparkles slightly, caused by residual gas in the wine giving it a slight effervescence.

Pulp fermentation   A method of fermenting the fruit pulp to obtain an extraction of colour and flavour.

Pulp sinker   A piece of equipment used to keep the fruit pulp below the surface of a fermenting must.

Punt   The 'dimple' in the base of a bottle, round which any sediment collects.

Racking   Transferring the wine from one container to another using a syphon.

Sediment   Solid particles which have been precipitated from the wine and settle on the bottom of the container.

Sparkling wine   A wine with residual gas content as a result of fermentation in the bottle.

Specific gravity   The specific gravity of a liquid is the weight of liquid of a given volume, compared with the weight of an equal volume of water at the same temperature.

Sticking fermentation   A condition which may occur, in which the wine stops fermenting prematurely, but may start again later.

Still wine   A wine with no residual carbon dioxide.

Tannin   The tannic acid content of wine; tannin gives wine astringency. There is more tannin in red wine than in white wine.

Vinegar   Produced in wine by contamination with airborne bacteria, sometimes referred to as acetobacter.

Wort   The mixture of ingredients from which beer is made.

Yeast   A microscopic fungus which causes fermentation.

Yeast nutrient   Salts which are used to stimulate yeast growth. The main salt is ammonium phosphate.

Yeast starter   A yeast culture which has been re-activated from its dormant state.

2

Equipment

One of the attractions of home wine making is its cheapness. There is therefore no point in buying a lot of expensive equipment at the start. If you begin by making small 1-gallon batches of wine you will have to buy very little. Then, as your experience and confidence grow, you can make larger batches and start to build up a collection of more sophisticated equipment. Doing it this way you will be sure that you do not buy equipment that never gets used, and you will have sufficient experience to pick out and discard the various gimmicky gadgets on the market that have little practical value.

Equipment for the beginner

A boiling vessel A large pan will be necessary for boiling the ingredients for some wines. It will need to be of about 2 gallons capacity, so a preserving pan of the sort used for jam making or fruit bottling will probably be best. It may be of stainless steel (in which case it could also be used as a fermentation vessel, see below), aluminium or unchipped enamelled iron; never use a copper or brass pan.

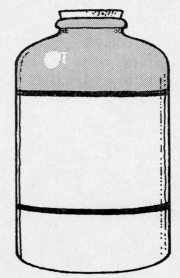

A wooden spoon Pick a large spoon with a long handle.

A fermentation vessel This is what holds the must while it ferments. The most suitable

A 2-gal. earthenware jar makes an ideal fermentation vessel

and easily obtained vessel for a beginner is a 2-gallon bucket made of heavy grade polythene or polypropylene. It should have a close fitting lid, which can be bored and fitted with an airlock to allow the escape of carbon dioxide. Remember, though, that plastic containers are intended for short term storage and should be used only for short periods of fermentation (say up to 4 weeks).

ALTERNATIVES

1. Glazed earthenware   This in fact is the ideal material for a fermentation vessel and as you progress with wine making you would be advised to buy earthenware vessels. They are much better than plastic for must which needs fermenting for longer periods. Cover the top of the vessel with a sheet of heavy gauge polythene (such as that supplied for use in home freezers), tied in place as tightly as possible with string or, on narrower necked jars, with a large rubber band. This will keep out contaminating bacteria but allow gases formed during fermentation to escape.

Glazed earthenware fermentation vessels are available either as open pans, varying in diameter from 1 ft. 6 in. to 3 ft. 6 in., or as bung mouthed jars. The latter are easier to use as the small opening is easier to cover effectively.

BUT take care that the pan you are using is made of modern, salt glazed earthenware. Older type pans were lead glazed; it is possible with these for the acid in the fermenting must to extract some of the lead from the glaze, leading to lead poisoning. The glazes are easily distinguished; lead glazing is opaque, honey coloured and dull in appearance while salt glaze is transparent, allowing the colour of the pan to show through. IF YOU HAVE THE SLIGHTEST DOUBT ABOUT THE GLAZE OF THE VESSEL, DO NOT USE IT.

2. Stainless steel   A stainless steel preserving pan may be used. NEVER use pans made of aluminium, copper, brass, iron or zinc for fermentation; with these metals there is a strong possibility of an interaction between the must and the metal which could lead to metal poisoning (aluminium pans may be used for boiling, see above). Again the top is covered with polythene, held in place with string.

3. Glass   Glass containers have the advantages of being easy to clean

1 White and red currants ready for picking.

2 Green gooseberries, suitable for a dry wine.

3 Ripe gooseberries for a sweet wine.

and allowing observation of the fermentation. However, if you use colourless glass, tie a piece of brown paper round the outside to protect the contents from the light, otherwise the wine may lose some of its colour.

DO NOT USE wooden casks for fermentation – they are difficult to handle and virtually impossible to clean sufficiently for continuing use. Casks may however make ideal storage vessels for maturing the wine (see pages 65–67).

Two 1-gallon storage jars with corks to fit Glass is the most common material for these jars but if colourless glass is used, the wine should be protected from the light with a piece of brown paper tied round the jar.

Cork stoppered stone jars are also used. These have the advantage of keeping the light from the wine, but they prevent observation and make it easy to leave the wine on the lees for too long after fermentation has stopped.

Plastic containers are sometimes used, but many plastics give the wine an 'off' taste and it is not worth risking this unless you have absolutely no alternative.

An airlock This is a device which prevents air and fruit flies from reaching the wine but which allows the gas formed during fermentation to escape. The neck of the storage jar is fitted with a cork; the seal between the cork and the jar must be perfect, but a hole is bored in the centre of the cork, into which a piece of glass or plastic tube is fitted – again the seal must be perfect so that the only escape route for gas, or entry route for air, is via the tube.

In a glass airlock the tube then continues into a U shape with a bubble on each side. The far end of the U tube is open. The bottom of the U, below the bubbles, is filled with water.

A plastic airlock consists of two round chambers, one fitting inside the other and filled one-third full with water.

The water in both types of airlock forms a seal preventing the access of air and fruit flies. The gas from the jar will escape through the lock, and will be seen as bubbles in the water. Fermentation is complete when

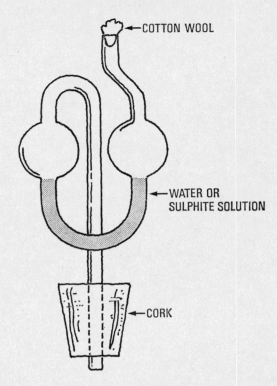

An airlock prevents air and fruit flies from reaching the wine but allows carbon dioxide to escape

the bubbles stop. This of course can be effective only if the seals between jar and cork and tube and cork are perfect.

Glass airlocks are expensive and easily broken. Plastic locks are more durable then glass but can split if carelessly handled, providing a harbour for undesirable organisms. The lock should therefore always be carefully inspected before use and discarded if it is not sound.

A measuring jug This may be glass, polythene or aluminium and should be calibrated in pints and fluid ounces. An ordinary 2-pint Pyrex kitchen measuring jug is ideal.

Kitchen scales Ordinary kitchen scales are usually adequate for weighing ingredients.

Funnel A large polythene funnel about 8-in. diameter is useful for pouring from one container to another.

Strainers A 6–8 in. diameter nylon sieve is ideal for straining pulp from the must. However, as this will not remove the finest particles, the must has to be strained again, through a cloth. A piece of blanket or fine meshed nylon is suitable for this. Letting the must drip through a jelly bag is not recommended as this takes a long time and exposes it to the air for too long.

Bottle brushes A small brush is needed for bottles and a larger one for gallon jars. A brush with nylon bristles and a wire handle is best, so that the handle will bend to reach stubborn deposits on the shoulders of the jar.

Tubing This is for syphoning the wine from one container to another. Use rubber or plastic tubing with $\frac{1}{4}$-in. bore, and have one or two lengths of about 3 ft. each.

Later on you will also need casks, bottles, corks and labels.

Equipment for the more advanced wine maker

Containers As you progress you will need to collect a supply of different sized fermentation vessels, from 1–5-gallon capacity, and larger storage jars such as 2-, 5- or 10-gallon carboys, all with corks to fit. You will also want additional airlocks for all the containers in use at one time.

Large carboys are difficult to handle when full and it is easiest to carry out the fermentation in the kitchen, where you can watch it, then syphon off the wine into buckets to transfer it to where you want to store it.

If you have difficulty obtaining corks that exactly fit your carboys, fasten a piece of polythene over the opening with a rubber band; a firm pad of cotton wool inserted into the mouth of the container will also provide an effective seal.

Measures Polythene buckets are useful for measuring large quantities and can be bought calibrated in both gallons and litres. A glass 4-fl. oz. measure is best for small quantities of acid and tannin solutions. A cylindrical glass measure with metric graduations is also very useful; this can also be used as a hydrometer jar.

Funnels   A 3-in. funnel is easier to use than the large one when filling bottles.

Bottle brushes   If carboys are to be used, a brush with 3-in. bristles and a handle not less than 2 ft. long will be required.

Tubing   For syphoning quantities of more than 5 gallons the tubing may have a bore of $\frac{3}{8}$ in., and with the larger container will need to be about 5 ft. long. Never go to a larger bore than $\frac{3}{8}$ in., though, as the lees may be drawn up into the syphon.

A hydrometer and jar   These are used for measuring the sugar content of a liquid and come in handy at several stages in wine making. A hydrometer consists of a glass stem about 8 in. long, with an elongated, bulbous end – it looks much like a fisherman's float. The stem contains a strip of paper on which are printed one or more graduated scales, and the bulbous end is weighted, so that it floats upright in the liquid being tested.

HOW A HYDROMETER WORKS:
The depth at which the hydrometer floats is determined by the amount of sugar present. The measurement shown by the instrument is referred to as specific gravity, usually noted as S.G. The specific weight of a liquid is defined as the weight of a given volume of that liquid compared with the weight of an equal volume of water under identical conditions. Water is the standard against which the S.G. is measured, marked on the hydrometer as 1.000.

For wine making purposes, the specific gravity figures above 1.000 are spoken of as 'gravity', and the figures below 1.000 as 'specific gravity'. The figures before the decimal point are dropped, so that a reading of 1.070 is called a gravity of 70, whilst a reading of 0.995 is called a specific gravity of .995 or minus 5.

The S.G. range encountered in wine making is usually between 0.990 and 1.100. A hydrometer with a range of 1.000 to 1.100 is therefore sufficient in most cases. Such a hydrometer will be marked up to 10 decimal points below 1.000. A second hydrometer with a range of 1.000 to 1.200 is useful for the occasions when the gravity exceeds 1.100.

As the stem of a hydrometer has only a small circumference, the fewer markings there are on the scale the easier it will be to read. Some

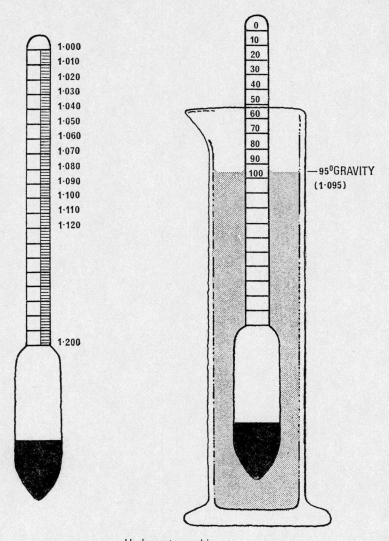

Hydrometer and jar

hydrometers have several scales, such as the S.G., the estimated alcohol content and the weight of sugar. Such instruments are very difficult to read as the scales have to overlap. Choose a hydrometer, therefore, with a single S.G. scale. A table relating S.G. to alcohol content is given on page 54.

Acid testing set   A simple acid testing set is available from equipment suppliers, together with full instructions. Details of when to use it are dealt with on page 47.

Fruit crushers   Small amounts of soft fruit may be crushed with a bottle with a flat base, in a polythene bucket. For larger quantities, use a small barrel with the head cut off, or a polythene bin, with a crusher made from hardwood. Hard fruits such as apples and pears are more difficult to crush. For these use a large mincer fitted with a plate with $\frac{1}{4}$-in. diameter holes. Alternatively, buy an inexpensive crusher.

Wine press   This is for extracting the juice from fruit pulp and pressing the juice out of the fermented must. A number of presses are available from specialist suppliers; they are rather expensive but very durable and if used carefully will last a lifetime. These presses are very efficient and provide good juice extraction.

Filters   Before the wine is bottled it may be passed through a series of filter materials which can be varied according to the amount of haze present in the wine. Filters can also be used for 'polishing' the wine – giving it brilliance. Several types of filter are available. They have a continuous action and are very efficient if used correctly. Asbestos pads are widely used as filters for commercial wines and spirits.

Corks and corking machines   A variety of corks will be needed for storage jars and bottles. There are two types of cork in general use; flanged stoppers are used for short periods of storage and for competitive exhibitions; bottles intended for longer storage, laid on their sides, should be corked with straight sided corks. Tapered corks should never be used for bottling wine.

Some wine makers use rubber bungs on fermentation and storage containers but this is not to be recommended as if they are allowed to come into contact with the wine for any length of time they may impart a rubbery flavour to it.

The corks can be driven into the bottles with a cork flogger or a wooden mallet; alternatively buy an inexpensive hand corking machine. If you are bottling large quantities it may even be worth buying a bench corker, which is efficient and will save a great deal of time and labour.

The bottle looks more professionally finished if the cork is covered with a metal foil or plastic capsule. These capsules come in a variety of colours and may be used to identify different types of wine. The metal foil capsule is fitted over the neck of the bottle with the help of a crimping ring. The plastic capsules are supplied in a container of liquid in which they must remain until used; the capsule is placed over the neck of the bottle and then left to dry and harden.

Labels   While a simple piece of gummed paper is adequate to identify the wine, attractive labels can be bought to decorate the bottles. Some wine makers even have their own personal labels printed.

Log book   A log book containing every detail of each batch of wine made is invaluable. If you know exactly what was done in previous years, it is soon possible to adjust a recipe and method until you have exactly the wine you want. The log book should contain the following information:

Date started
Type and quantity of ingredients
Variety of yeast used
Quantity of water
Quantity and type of sugar
Amount of yeast nutrient
Amount of tannin (if any)
Amount and type of acid used (if any)
Amount and variety of pectin reducing enzyme
Method of preparation of ingredients
Type of sterilisation of the must
Specific gravity of the must
Date of adding the yeast
Date of start of fermentation
Length of pulp fermentation
Weekly hydrometer readings, with dates
Date when fermentation ceased
Final hydrometer reading
Date of first racking
State of clarification (very cloudy, cloudy, slight haze, almost clear, etc.)
Dates of subsequent rackings
Date when wine finally cleared
Any other interesting factors, such as condition of fruit, whether the fruit was home grown, weather conditions prevailing during the growing and ripening seasons

Weather conditions and time of day when the fruit was gathered
Any problems encountered during fermentation or storage and the methods
used to overcome them
Whether the wine was fined or filtered
Assessment of the wine after 1 year

If you keep a log book meticulously for the first few years, this is the
best way to learn; there is no better guide than personal experience.

Care of equipment

Strict cleanliness must be maintained at all times with wine making
equipment. Everything should be well washed and sterilised both before
and after use. Any trace of wine or pulp left on equipment makes a perfect
breeding ground for spoilage organisms that will attack your next batch.

It is advisable to keep a stock of sulphite solution for sterilising
equipment, to save having to make a fresh solution each time it is
required. Make up the solution as follows:

Dissolve 2 oz. sodium metabisulphite in 10 fl. oz. warm water. When
the crystals have dissolved, add a further 10 fl. oz. cold water.

Use the solution in the proportion one part solution to eight parts
water. Add ½ tsp. citric acid to each 2 pints dilute solution before use.

Throughout this book, this solution will be referred to as sulphite
solution B. It should be used for sterilising all equipment.

3

Ingredients 1

Fruit, vegetables, flowers, dried fruit, herbs, grain and leaves

Fermented drink can be made from almost any non-poisonous plant, but the first secret is the selection of the right plant. There is no doubt that the best quality wines are made from fresh fruits. All wine makers experiment at some time with other ingredients – vegetables, dried fruits, flowers, herbs, grains – and often make quite acceptable wines. But all these plants lack at least one of the essential elements in a good fermentation – sugar, tannin and acid. Where one of these is lacking it has to be added artificially and the result is never quite as good as when all are present naturally.

What type of wine do you want?

Beginners should start by deciding whether to make a table wine, a sweet wine or a dessert wine. Whether a wine is dry or sweet depends on the amount of residual sugar after fermentation is complete. This in turn is governed by the initial sugar content of the must, including any additions of sugar made for a sweet wine, and by the efficiency of the fermentation. The quantity of sugar added is adjusted after considera- tion of the natural sugar content of the fruit used. It is therefore *possible* to make a dry or a sweet wine from any of the basic ingredients, but a little experience will show that most fruits and flavours lend themselves better to either one or the other.

Table wines, to drink with food, should have a delicate bouquet and flavour compatible with foods. Whether they are dryer or sweeter is a matter of choice, though very sweet wines are rarely the best with food. For table wines, peaches, apricots, apples, oranges, lemons, blackberries, elderberries, bilberries, red and white currants, pears, cherries, unripe gooseberries (see page 97) and of course grapes are among the most suitable ingredients.

Strongly flavoured wines are best kept as sweet or dessert wines. Raspberry wine, for instance, has a strong smell and flavour which make it unsuitable for drinking with meat and fish, so it is best made as a sweet wine for drinking after dinner. Grain wines, made from wheat, barley and rice, also have strong flavours and lend themselves better to the production of sweet wines. All these factors must be considered before deciding which type of wine to make.

A table of ingredients and the wine types they produce is shown opposite.

Fruit

Fruit for wine making must be sound, free from blemish and fully ripened on the plant. This means that bought fruit is not as good for wine as that grown at home – commercial fruit growers have to pick before the fruit is completely ripe so that it will withstand packing and transportation; the fruit continues to ripen after picking but the process is altered. Fruit ripened off the plant may be perfectly acceptable for eating but will not make the best wines. The only way to ensure that fruit is in first class condition and fully ripe when gathered is to grow it yourself. Most wine makers are therefore also gardeners.

Most fruit indigenous to Britain has a high acid and low sugar content. As the fruit ripens, the acidity drops and the sugar content rises. The wine maker must wait to pick it until it reaches the peak of ripeness; at this stage the acid content is at its lowest and the sugar content at its highest point. For example, red and white currants change colour quite early in the ripening process. They must be left on the bush for up to 4 weeks after they have changed colour before they will be ripe enough for wine (page 92). Wine made from fruit that is not thoroughly ripe will tend to have a 'green' characteristic in both bouquet and flavour. The illustrations facing pages 16, 17, 32 and 33 show certain fruits at their peak of ripeness; study these pictures and compare your own fruits with them before picking.

Pick all fruit on a dry, sunny day. If the weather is wet and humid, the skin of the fruit will be heavily contaminated with mould spores and bacteria, giving a high risk of disorders in the finished wine. In the case of soft fruits such as raspberries, strawberries and blackberries, the

FRUIT	DRY	MEDIUM	SWEET	DESSERT
Apple	V/good	Good	Good	Fair
Apricot	Good	Good	Good	Good
Bilberry	V/good	Good	Good	V/good
Blackberry	V/good	Good	Good	V/good
Bullace	Poor	Fair	Good	Fair
Cherry	V/good	Good	Good	V/good
White currant	V/good	Good	Good	Poor
Red currant	V/good	V/good	Good	Poor
Black currant	Not good	Fair	Fair	Poor
Elderberry	V/good	Good	Good	V/good
Gooseberry (green)	Excellent	Good	Poor	Not good
Gooseberry (ripe)	Not good	Fair	Good	Good
Grape (White)	Excellent	Excellent	Excellent	Excellent
Grape (Red)	Excellent	Good	Good	Ex. as Port-type
Grapefruit	Good	Good	Good	Not good
Greengage	Fair	Good	Good	Fair
Lemon	V/good	Good	Good	Poor
Loganberry	Fair	Good	Good	Good
Mulberry	Not good	Fair	Good	Poor
Orange	V/good	Good	Good	Fair
Tangerine	Good	Good	Good	Fair
Peach	V/good	Good	Good	Good
Pear	Good	Good	Good	Fair
Pineapple	Poor	Fair	Good	Poor
Plum	Fair	Good	Good	Good
Damson	Fair	Fair	Good	Good
Raspberry	Not good	Fair	Good	Fair
Rhubarb	Good	Good	Good	Poor
Sloe	Good	Good	Good	Fair
Strawberry	Poor	Fair	Good	Fair

flavour is much better if the fruit is picked in brilliant sunshine after a sunny spell.

Exactly the same procedure is adopted in the fine vineyards of France and Germany. The vintner waits and watches until the grapes reach the correct degree of ripeness before gathering them. In some cases, where the best sweet wines are made, the grapes are not harvested all at once but selected bunches are left on the vine until they start to turn brown and soft with sugar. These give the finest, rich dessert wines of Sauternes and the Rhine valley.

Preparation of the fruit

Detach small fruits such as currants and elderberries from their stalks with the fingers. It is possible to use a table fork for this, but the fingers are more sensitive and less likely to pull off any fine stalks which, if included in the wine, would give it a 'stemmy' taste. Fingers, too, will detect any unripe berries in the cluster, which should be discarded. These soft fruits and berries can then be crushed by hand using a bottle or wooden crusher (page 22).

Plums, damsons, apricots and peaches should be stoned before use if possible; if the flesh adheres firmly to the stones, ferment the pulp for 24 hours and then remove the stones – fermentation will break down the flesh so that the stones can be removed more easily. If the stones are left in too long during fermentation, the flavour of the kernels may be leached into the wine, making it taste of almonds. Hard fruits such as apples, pears and green gooseberries are very difficult to crush and for these use a coarse mincer; a plate with $\frac{1}{4}$-in. diameter holes is about right. After mincing, some of these fruits are fermented as pulp and some are put through a press to extract the juice. Grapes can also be put through the mincer, which crushes the fruit effectively without crushing the pips.

Vegetables

Parsnips and carrots are still widely used for wine. Other vegetables such as turnips, beans, kohl rabi, spinach, lettuce etc. can be used, but the results are so poor that wines – or fermented drinks – from such ingredients are rapidly disappearing from the home wine maker's cellar. Beetroot is often used but it tends to have an earthy flavour; this may be kept to a minimum if young, small beetroots are used.

Wine made from potatoes has the reputation of being very potent. Potatoes tend to produce a wine with a relatively high methyl alcohol content which should be treated with caution. Green potatoes should never be used. If the tuber is allowed to go green through exposure to light a toxic glycoside called solanine will be produced; this substance is insoluble in water, will withstand boiling, and is very poisonous.

Preparation of the vegetables

Vegetables require a somewhat different treatment from fruit. As the roots are hard, it is necessary to boil them in order to extract the flavour. As they are highly flavoured, it is best to boil them in an open pan to allow the volatile substances to escape with the steam. So, peel and wash the vegetables thoroughly, cut them into small pieces and cook them in unsalted water until they are tender and can be pierced easily with a fork. Remove the pan from the heat and strain off the liquid without pressing the vegetables; discard the vegetables (or eat them!). Do not overboil during cooking as this will make the wine difficult to clear.

As vegetables have very little sugar, acid, yeast nutrient or tannin, these have to be added to the must before fermentation.

Flowers

The petals of some flowers make very attractive wines. They will necessarily be light wines with a delicate, aromatic bouquet. In the case of rose petal wine, made from red roses, the colour is also very attractive. However, as flower petals are lacking in acid, sugar and yeast nutrient the rate of yeast growth will be slow and fermentation incomplete unless these deficiencies are first rectified. Some flowers are also deficient in tannin and this will need to be adjusted. The flowers most commonly used for wines are red roses, elderflowers, cowslips and dandelions. Coltsfoot, marigolds, clover, carnations and primroses can also be used.

Generally speaking you will need 3–4 pints of petals to make a gallon of wine, pressing the petals very lightly into the measuring container. If you want a more robust wine than will be provided by the petals alone, add ½ lb. sultanas or ½ pint grape concentrate, but remember that the flavour will be slightly altered by these additions. When removing the petals from any flower head, take great care not to include any of the green parts as these give the wine an 'off' flavour.

Preparation of the must for a flower wine

There are two ways of producing the must for a flower wine. The first is to put the petals in a container, pour on boiling water and leave to infuse for 24 hours. The must is then strained and the acid and tannin content adjusted. For the second method, a must is prepared from all the ingredients *except* the flower petals; the yeast is added and allowed to ferment for 5 days. The petals are added at this stage and allowed to ferment for 3 days before straining.

The first method is the simplest but many of the volatile compounds in the flowers are lost by the use of hot water, and the bouquet of the wine is deprived of some of its vitality. The second method produces a better wine but has to be very carefully controlled.

ROSE PETAL WINE

Wine made from rose petals should be medium sweet or sweet. It matures quickly and will be at its best after 18 months. It will usually start to deteriorate after 2 years, though of course there are always exceptions. Some varieties of rose are highly perfumed and these varieties should be used with care as too much perfume in the wine is undesirable. Keep quantities to a minimum, using no more than 4 pints of loosely packed petals per gallon. One of the best roses for a red wine is Ena Harkness; this will give a wine with a lovely colour.

Gather the petals when the flowers are fully opened and the petals are just on the verge of dropping. Discard any brown parts on the petals as these will give the wine a bitter taste.

ELDERFLOWER WINE

A well balanced, dry wine made from elderflowers is quite acceptable but they lend themselves better to a medium dry or medium sweet wine.

There are several varieties of elderflower, not all of which make good wine. Some varieties give a wine with a distinctly unpleasant smell; this can usually be detected as a bad smell in the flowers before they are picked, so do check this first. In any case, avoid flowers from the tree elder and varieties on which the flower umbels are small. Large quantities of flowers from any variety tend to produce this same unpleasant smell, so never use more than $\frac{3}{4}$–1 pint of petals per gallon. Pick the flowers when they look white and frothy, like the head on a pint of beer. They should be fully opened but not faded. It is better to pick the petals straight from the bush into the measuring jug than to gather the whole umbels and pick off the petals at home. The petals come off more easily when the flowers are absolutely fresh and there is less likelihood of stalks getting into the must. Never press the petals into the measuring jug.

Dried elderflowers can be bought from many wine equipment shops. These should be used in the proportion $\frac{1}{2}$ oz. flowers per gallon. However, wine made from dried elderflowers will always be inferior to a wine made from fresh flowers.

COWSLIP WINE

Cowslips make a very pleasant wine, though unfortunately these days it is difficult to find enough cowslips.

Cowslip wine should be made as a medium sweet wine, and will improve with age. It has the reputation of being a mild soporific; country people used firmly to believe that a glass of cowslip wine taken before retiring ensured a good night's sleep. Wine can be made from both fresh and dried cowslips, though fresh flowers make the better wine.

DANDELION WINE

This is still made but has lost a lot of its former popularity, probably because it is difficult to make a really good dandelion wine. As with elderflowers, it is important not to use too many petals or the wine acquires an unpleasant smell. Not more than 4 pints of loosely packed petals should be used per gallon, and the wine should be made medium sweet or sweet.

Gather the flowers in full sunshine when they are fully open. Pick the petals from the dandelion head, leaving behind all green parts; if the latter are included in the must the wine will have a green bouquet and a bitter flavour.

Dried fruits

All dried fruits, such as dates, figs, raisins and sultanas, have a high sugar content. In order to produce wines from them successfully the sugar content must be known accurately, which means that a hydrometer must be used. To make the must, boil the fruit in a small quantity of water and press it well. Wash the pulp in a little hot water, press again, add this to the first pressing and make up the concentrated liquor to 1 gallon with more water. Discard the pulp and measure the sugar content of the must before you start fermentation. Extract prepared this way will be prone to pectin haze and a pectinase enzyme will have to be added; the acidity of the must will also have to be adjusted.

Herbs

The most popular herbs for wine making are parsley, tea and lemon balm. Other herbs may be used but the wine made is of doubtful quality.

PARSLEY WINE

To prepare parsley for wine making, strip the curly leaves from the stalks and discard the stalks. If the stalks are included they give the wine an overpowering flavour. Wash the leaves well, put them in a container and pour boiling water over. After infusing it for 24 hours, strain the must through a cloth and press lightly. Parsley is deficient in acid, sugar and yeast nutrient, so these will have to be added to the must, and a little tannin will also improve the wine.

LEMON BALM WINE

This is made from the young growing tips of the herbs, gathered when the plant is in full growth. The method of preparation is the same as for parsley.

TEA WINE

The best tea wine is made from China tea; it is delicate in flavour and has an enchanting bouquet. There is plenty of tannin in tea, but acid, sugar and yeast nutrient will have to be added, together with a pectinase enzyme to help clarification.

4 Elderberries, just ready for wine making.

5 Peach wine is second only to a grape wine.

Grain

Wines made from grain have the reputation of being high in alcohol. This is because they tend to smell like spirits, which gives a misleading impression of a high alcohol content. However, they certainly have the colour of whisky or brandy and may have something of the flavour. Grains used by themselves do not make very palatable wine and raisins or sultanas are usually added to give a better flavour.

Wheat and barley are sometimes contaminated by vermin, so it is important to select only good, clean samples for wine making. When using rice, choose the best quality, clean Patna rice. Be careful that the grain is not broken or crushed in any way; if any of the grain is broken a very cloudy wine with a lot of starch haze is produced and rice in particular becomes very difficult to handle. To produce the must, pour boiling water over the grain and ferment on the grain. As there is very little acid in grain, the acidity of the must will have to be adjusted.

Grains are best used for a medium sweet or sweet wine, and all grain wines improve tremendously with keeping. Wheat and raisin is probably the most pleasing mixture and after a good maturation period of, say, 15 years can be very smooth and full bodied, a heavy wine to drink with caution. The longer you keep grain wines the better they will be.

Rice wine is sometimes referred to as 'sake' but this is not accurate. Sake is produced in Japan and China by fermenting rice with indigenous mould and yeast; our own rice wine can never be the same.

Leaves

Oak leaves have been used in wine making with varying degrees of success, but it is important not to use too many leaves. The leaves have a high tannin content and if used too freely will give too much astringency; 4 pints per gallon is plenty.

Gather the leaves in autumn, pour 1 gallon boiling water over them and leave to stand for 24 hours. Strain the must, adjust the acidity and gravity and add yeast nutrient; ½ lb. chopped sultanas added to the must will improve the flavour.

Wine can also be made from the prunings of grape vines, using leaves and tendrils in the proportion 4 lb. per gallon. Cover the prunings with boiling water and leave to soak for 48 hours. Strain the must, adjust the acidity and add sugar and a pectinase enzyme. This is often called 'folly' wine, from the French 'feuillage'.

Sterilisation of the must

All main ingredients used in wine making should be sterilised when the must has been prepared. Fruit especially has numerous wild yeasts, mould spores and bacteria on the skins and unless these are destroyed before the fermentation commences they will cause disorders in the wine. The must can be sterilised by boiling the ingredients, pouring boiling water over them, or by the use of sodium metabisulphite. This can be purchased in bulk, or in the form of Campden tablets.

Boiling the ingredients is necessary for vegetable and dried fruit wines, herbs and flowers have boiling water poured over them, but all fresh fruit should be sterilised by the use of sulphite. Campden tablets have the advantage of being handy to use; they should be crushed before use. A cheaper way of using sulphite is to make up a solution using $\frac{1}{2}$ oz. sodium metabisulphite to 20 fl. oz. water. This will be referred to as sulphite solution A. It is used in the proportion 1 fl. oz. to 1 gallon. Fruit should not be boiled or the wine may have a cooked taste, and boiling will destroy a lot of the volatile compounds in the fruit, thus robbing the wine of a lot of bouquet and flavour.

4

Ingredients 2

Yeasts, sugars and water

Yeast

Yeast is a microscopic fungus which causes fermentation. Men used it for thousands of years, to make light bread and fermented drinks, without understanding how it worked. During the nineteenth century, however, it came under the scrutiny of scientists and certain strains are now cultivated on a commercial basis. The use of cultivated yeasts enables us to control the fermentation to produce exactly the desired results in our wine, beer, mead or bread; there are many, many strains of wild yeast but the object of the modern brewer or wine maker is to eliminate these from his must so that he can fully control the fermentation. The exception is the maker of fine grape wines, who makes use of the exceptional yeasts naturally forming on the skins of the grapes.

How yeast works

A yeast cell can be seen only through a microscope; 5000 cells placed side by side span 1 inch. Each cell contains a great number of enzymes, some of which control the fermentation. (An enzyme has the capacity to bring about a change in a substance without being changed itself.) For example, the enzyme invertase breaks down sucrose into fermentable sugars; the enzyme amylase performs a similar task on starch.

The yeast cells feed on the sugars in the must, which their own enzymes help to supply, and multiply. As they feed on the sugars they convert them partly into alcohol, partly into gases; the gases escape from the fermenting must, the alcohol remains in it. Eventually the alcohol concentration becomes so high that the yeast cells can no longer survive; they are destroyed and fermentation stops.

Cultivated yeasts will withstand quite large amounts of alcohol – up to 15 or 18 per cent by volume (expressed as % v/v) – before they die;

wild yeasts on the other hand will usually give up at about 4% v/v, producing a very poor wine.

Cultivated yeasts

The two cultivated yeasts most widely used are Saccharomyces Cerivisiae and Saccharomyces Torula. Strains from Sacc. Torula are used chiefly in animal fodders, and it is with Sacc. Cerivisiae that we are concerned. This may be bought as granulated bakers' yeast, moist bakers' yeast, moist brewers' yeast or selected wine yeasts; the latter come in liquid or tablet form or on agar slopes. The wine yeasts were originally intended for use in the commercial wine trade and are still used during bad seasons when the conditions for harvesting grapes are poor and the natural yeasts adhering to them are unhealthy. Amateur wine makers have the benefit of research carried out for the professional users over seventy years.

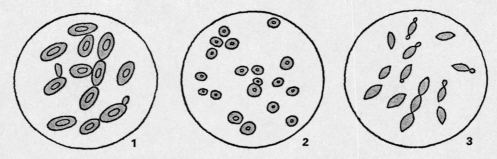

Yeast cells as seen through a microscope.
1. Sacc. Ellipsoidus (wine yeast). 2. Sacc. Cerivisiae (bakers' yeast). 3. Apiculata (wild yeast).

Wine yeasts

Sacc. Cerivisiae, variety Ellipsoidus, is the yeast generally used for fermenting in the wine producing countries. It is therefore the obvious choice of the amateur wine maker who wishes to control his wine making and produce good quality wines. There are many strains of this yeast and they are generally referred to as 'selected wine yeasts'. Some of the strains available are port, sherry, Malaga, Madeira, Sauternes, Tokay, Pommard, Bordeaux (claret), Champagne, Burgundy, Chablis, and there is also an all purpose yeast. A cereal wine yeast can be used for fermenting grain wines.

The various strains of wine yeast take their names from the regions where they predominate; for example, Burgundy yeast in the Côte d'Or, port yeast in the Douro valley. Over the centuries these yeasts have adapted themselves to the particular environment of that area. In its natural habitat, a certain strain of yeast will confer some of its characteristics to the wine of that region. Some will influence the wine more than others, but all play an important part in giving the wine its particular flavour and bouquet. The yeast, however, is only one of several factors involved in giving these wines their individual character; the variety of grapes used, the soil and climate in which they are grown and the method of wine production all play a part. A special wine yeast, when used for fermenting ingredients other than grapes grown in a specific region, will not produce a wine resembling that of the region. For instance, a Burgundy yeast used for fermenting elderberries will not produce a Burgundy wine. Nevertheless by skilful preparation of the must, and by use of a red wine yeast, it is possible to produce an acceptable table wine to be used in place of a Burgundy.

Using a selected wine yeast has everything in its favour. It will ensure an efficient and complete fermentation and this will be a quiet, uniform process compared to the more spectacular fermentation of bakers' yeast. It will produce maximum colour extraction from red ingredients. Under favourable conditions, selected wine yeasts are able to produce 16–18% v/v alcohol. Some yeasts are even able to produce as much as 21% v/v. As most of the wine produced by amateur wine makers is between 11% and 14% v/v alcohol, this is well within the limits of the yeast's capabilities. Any flavour imparted to the wine by the yeast will be a good one. If a sedimentary wine yeast has been used, the lees will settle to a firm deposit thus making racking easy and so lessen the amount of wastage.

A few strains of wine yeast tend to autolyse easily. These are the more powdery yeasts and include Malaga, Madeira and port yeasts. These should not be used in the preparation of red table wine as they may affect its colour and are better for dessert wines. Red table wines are best fermented with Burgundy, Bordeaux or Pommard yeasts. Pommard yeast especially will give maximum colour from red ingredients.

For dry white wine use either a hock, Chablis or an all purpose yeast. For sweet wines, use Sauternes, Tokay, or Lacrima Christi; a Sauternes yeast will also impart a slight sweetness to a dry wine.

Sherry type wines are best fermented with a sherry yeast. These yeasts will impart some sherry flavour to the wine if it is matured with an air space in the container. The alcohol content of a sherry type wine should not be less than 15% v/v, or the wine may become infected by bacteria during storage. It may therefore be advisable to add spirit such as brandy to the wine, increasing the alcohol content to 18% v/v to protect it from bacterial action.

For port type wines a port yeast is the best to use. The production of commercial port is a complicated process which the amateur wine maker cannot hope to emulate, and he should not expect too much from his efforts. Nevertheless, palatable port type wines can be made from black-berries, elderberries, loganberries and damsons. As port, like sherry, is a fortified wine, the addition of brandy up to 18% v/v alcohol will improve it.

Sparkling wines may be made using a Champagne yeast. This is not essential, however, for the average wine maker wishing to make a sparkling wine can get satisfactory results from a good, sedimentary, all purpose yeast.

Using other yeasts – baker's yeast

Bakers' yeast will start a fermentation quickly but will not produce good quality wine. It will easily ferment invert sugar and sucrose but, having been cultivated in an almost alcohol-free environment, will not immedi-ately tolerate a high concentration of alcohol. Once an appreciable amount of alcohol is formed, fermentation slows right down, the dead yeast cells autolyse and form yeast nutrient; this stimulates a slow yeast growth and fermentation will continue at a very slow rate. Wine made with bakers' yeast can therefore ferment for a very long time and will have a strong yeasty flavour that will stay with the wine for many months. In addition to this, bakers' yeasts, both moist and granulated, are floc-culent yeasts which will not settle firmly on the bottom of the vessel after fermentation; this means that a lot of wine will be lost during racking.

Brewers' yeast

Brewers' yeast is produced in a hopped must, and this will impart a bitter taste to the finished drink; it is therefore not suitable for making wine, but is of course ideal for beer. It is a mixture of powdery and flocculent yeasts of the species Sacc. Cerivisiae. Brewers' yeasts are usually top fermenters which will develop a head on the surface of the fermenting must, making it difficult to carry out racking efficiently. They are also intolerant to high concentrations of alcohol – yeast growth is inhibited slightly even in a 1% alcohol solution and fermentation will not usually proceed beyond 9% v/v alcohol. The yeast used in lager production, Sacc. Carlsbergensis, is a bottom fermenter, but this yeast is best reserved for making lager.

Wild yeasts

In wine making terminology any yeast which is not cultivated is called a wild yeast. There are still wine recipes in existence which do not specify the addition of yeast and these rely for fermentation on the wild yeasts present in the ingredients, or airborne yeasts which settle on the must. Any must prepared from fresh fruits will start to ferment naturally unless first sterilised; the cause is wild yeasts which start to ferment very quickly. Since we have no control over the action of wild yeasts these should be eliminated. The only method of producing good quality wine is to sterilise the must and then to inoculate it with a selected wine yeast. In established vineyards in good wine areas, the yeast on the grapes is good and no additional yeast is added to the must, but even grapes, if grown in this country, are better sterilised and inoculated with a cultivated yeast.

Wild yeasts are quickly inhibited by weak concentrations of alcohol and will seldom produce more than 4% v/v alcohol. They tend to produce relatively large amounts of acetic acid, as much as 1·2 grams per litre, whereas the selected wine yeasts will produce at most 0·6 grams per litre. The high acetic acid content will give the wine a vinegary tang which will remain fairly constant throughout its life. Unpleasant esters are also formed which give the wine disagreeable flavours, such as a bitterness which only becomes apparent after drinking. Wild yeasts will often give the wine a muddy appearance, making clarification difficult, and are often accompanied by spoilage bacteria and moulds which can take over and spoil the wine.

Yeast nutrient

The pure undiluted juice of grapes and most other fruits will contain sufficient yeast nutrient to feed the cells and start them multiplying.

However, since most fruit juices are used diluted with water, the must is often deficient in yeast nutrient; in any case the natural nutrients are not always available to the yeasts without the help of added salts. It is therefore usual to add a yeast nutrient to the must. If sufficient nutrient is already available in the must, the small amount added will affect neither the quality nor the flavour of the wine. But without an adequate supply of nutrient it is impossible to ensure good reproduction of yeast cells in the lag phase or the replacement of dead cells during fermentation; the result would be an incomplete fermentation, stopping before sufficient alcohol were produced, giving a very sweet, cordial type wine.

Yeast nutrient is available from suppliers of wine making equipment. Choose one with a high proportion of ammonium phosphate and use it according to the directions on the pack. If, after you have added the nutrient to the must, fermentation still appears sluggish, it may be necessary to add a yeast energiser. This will certainly be the case with musts prepared from dried fruits, or canned or concentrated fruit juices; these, and musts produced from a small quantity of ingredients, will all be low in the necessary vitamins. Yeast growth is assisted by the addition of a small amount of vitamin B1. This can be bought in 3-milligram tablets, and half a tablet is enough for 1 gallon of must. Alternatively, add 1 level tsp. Marmite per gallon (Marmite is based on yeast extract and is rich in B group vitamins).

Preparing a yeast starter

Once the must is made, it is important to start fermentation quickly. The longer the must is quiescent, the greater the risk of contamination by moulds and bacteria. If the yeast culture is added directly to the must it may take perhaps a week to become active; it is normal therefore to prepare a 'starter'. This consists basically of a small bottle of sterile liquid containing a good balance of yeast nutrients and energisers, to which the yeast culture is added 2–3 days before it will be required for a must. The yeast starts to ferment in this small bottle and is already active when added to the must.

Pre-activation of the yeast also safeguards against adding a dud culture to the must, which would inevitably develop mould growth, and against adding a contaminated culture. If a culture in a starter bottle shows no signs of starting to ferment, or if there is evidence of contamination by micro-organisms, the starter *and* the rest of that batch of culture should be discarded.

A starter is very easy to prepare. As a yeast culture can be easily contaminated, take care to ensure that the starter medium is sterile. The medium is prepared especially for the rapid growth of yeast, but it is also an ideal breeding ground for moulds and spoilage bacteria which, if allowed access to the medium, would multiply very quickly. Sterilise the bottle for the starter with sulphite solution B (page 24) and rinse it several times with boiled water to remove all traces of the sulphite; then plug the mouth with cotton wool to prevent re-contamination. Sterilise the medium by boiling.

4 fl. oz. freshly strained orange juice sweetened with $\frac{1}{2}$ oz. sugar makes a suitable medium. Bring the mixture to the boil in a closed pan, cool it to 70°F (21°C) and pour it into the sterile bottle. Add the yeast culture, re-insert the cotton wool plug and put the bottle in a warm place for 2–3 days until it starts to ferment.

If you have a pressure cooker it may be convenient to prepare a small stock of starter bottles. You will need six small screw cap bottles of about 8-fl. oz. capacity. Small bottles in which soft drinks are sold are ideal. Wash the bottles and caps thoroughly, sterilise them with sulphite solution, rinse them several times with water and replace the caps. Then prepare the starter medium.

YEAST STARTER MEDIUM

$1\frac{1}{2}$ pt. (0·8 l.) water
$1\frac{1}{2}$ oz. (45 g.) sugar
1 tbsp. malt extract
1 level tsp. ammonium phosphate B.P.
$\frac{1}{2}$ level tsp. citric acid
$\frac{1}{2}$ level tsp. Marmite

Bring all the ingredients to the boil in a closed pan and allow to cool. Measure the liquid and make it up to $1\frac{1}{2}$ pints with boiled water, if necessary. Pour $\frac{1}{4}$ pint solution into each bottle and plug them with non-absorbent cotton wool. Do not replace the caps at this stage.

Remove the baskets from the pressure cooker and invert the trivet. Fold a piece of cloth and place it on the trivet, so that the bottles will not touch the metal. Put 1 pint water into the cooker and load it with the six bottles, placing a piece of folded newspaper between and round the bottles to make sure they do not touch each other or the sides of the pan. Bring the cooker slowly to 15 lb. pressure and maintain at pressure for 15 minutes. Remove the cooker from the heat and allow the pressure to drop at room temperature. Do not reduce the pressure by placing the pan in cold water.

Remove the bottles and, leaving the cotton wool plugs in place, screw on the caps tightly. The bottles can now be stored in the refrigerator or a cool place until required. They will keep for at least a year.

To bring a starter bottle into use, pour the yeast culture into the bottle and immediately replace the cotton wool plug. Shake the bottle and put it in a warm place (70°F, 21°C) to start working.

Sugar

The best sugar to use in wine making is white cane or beet sugar. This sugar is sold today in a very pure form and further treatment of it is unnecessary. The types of sugar that concern the wine maker may be divided into fermentable and non-fermentable sugars.

Fermentable sugars

Sucrose – cane or beet sugar
Glucose or Dextrose
Fructose or fruit sugar, sometimes called levulose
Invert sugar – This is a mixture of glucose and fructose and is obtained by enzymatic hydrolysis of sucrose. The term 'invert sugar' originates from the fact that when sucrose is converted into glucose and levulose by the enzyme invertase, the rotation of the polarised light is changed to the opposite direction. That is to say sucrose rotates polarised light to the right, whereas invert sugar rotates it to the left.

All of these sugars are readily fermented by the yeast Sacc. Cerivisiae. Granulated sugar is fairly inexpensive, gives no significant flavour to the wine, and produces no 'off' flavours during fermentation. Invert sugar is more expensive, and as the wine yeasts also contain the enzyme which converts the ordinary sugars very efficiently, there seems no point in buying it. Some wine makers prefer to use invert sugar in preference to sucrose, claiming that it ferments more readily than sucrose, and that sucrose does not ferment out to dryness. Controlled experiments prove this to be a fallacy.

Other grades of sugar are Demerara, moist brown sugar and Barbados. As these sugars will deepen the colour of the wine and alter its flavour, giving it a caramellised taste, they are best avoided in wine making.

Non-fermentable sugars
Lactose or milk sugar.
This is the only non-fermentable sugar that we need to concern ourselves with. This sugar is not fermented by Sacc. Cerivisiae, although other members of the Saccharomyces family can ferment it, because they contain the necessary lactose which the Cerivisiae lacks. This makes lactose a suitable sugar to use for sweetening a finished wine as there is no danger of the wine re-fermenting through the addition of sugar. Unfortunately lactose has only about one-third the sweetening power of sucrose.

Honey
Another sweetening agent, containing both dextrose and levulose, is honey. This can be used in place of sucrose. As honey contains flavouring substances, its use is better confined to the production of mead (page 146).

Adding sugar to the must
When adding sugar to a fermenting wine, it is better to add it as a heavy syrup. Make this by dissolving 1 lb. sugar in ½ pint boiling water. This will give a syrup with a gravity of 300 (1.300 – page 20). Sugar added in this form is more easily dispersed in bulk. If sugar is added in dry form, there is a danger that some will settle on the bottom of the container and form a dense layer; this will seriously impede yeast growth, possibly destroying live yeast cells, which will have a disastrous effect on the fermentation. Take care not to add too much sugar to the must initially. The starting gravity of a must should never exceed 100 (1.100).

When adjusting the must prior to fermentation, it is necessary to know the residual sugar present, obtained from the ingredients used. Some basic ingredients contain a large amount of natural sugar, and unless this is taken into consideration when the must is being prepared, too much sugar may be added, with adverse effects. A simple but effective method of calculating the amount of sugar syrup needed is by the use of the Pearson Square. To employ the Pearson Square, the gravity of the must and that of the sugar syrup must be known. The sugar syrup is made by dissolving 1 lb. of sugar in ½ pint water. This will give a syrup with an approximate gravity of 300.

Gravity of Syrup		Parts of Syrup	
A 300		B 50	
	Desired Gravity E 100		$\dfrac{50}{200} = \dfrac{1}{4}$
50 C		200 D	
Gravity of Must		Parts of Must	

The Pearson Square is employed as follows:
1. The top left hand corner (A) shows the gravity of the sugar syrup.
2. The top right hand corner (B) shows the parts of syrup needed to give the desired gravity.
3. The bottom left hand corner (C) shows the gravity of the must.
4. The bottom right hand corner (D) shows the required parts of must.
5. The centre of the square (E) shows the desired gravity.
   The desired gravity is deducted from the gravity of the sugar syrup (A–E) the resulting figure is then entered in the bottom right hand corner (D).

The gravity of the must (C) is deducted from the desired gravity (E–C) and the resulting figure is entered in the top right hand corner (B).

This is a simple way of calculating how many parts of sugar syrup need to be added to the parts of must to achieve the desired gravity

$$B = \frac{E-C}{A-E}$$ The ratio in the shown example is one part of syrup to 4 parts of must. $$B = \frac{100 - 50}{300 - 100} = \frac{50}{200} = \frac{1}{4}$$

Expressed in terms of ounces, 1 fl. oz. syrup is needed for each 4 fl. oz. must. There are 160 fl. oz. in a gallon, and 32 fl. oz. of syrup (1) added to 128 fl. oz. of must (4) would give this volume.

The total capacity of a 1-gallon storage jar is about 180 fl. oz. In order to avoid an air space in the jar, a volume more than 1 gallon is needed. In this case, 36 fl. oz. syrup (1) and 144 fl. oz. of must (4) would give a total volume of 180 fl. oz. with a gravity of 100.

Water

In almost every case it is necessary to add water to the must and, generally speaking, tap water is perfectly satisfactory. The exceptions are recently chlorinated water or excessively hard water. Water that has been chlorinated will adversely affect the flavour of the wine, giving it an iodine or disinfectant characteristic. Boiling the water will disperse some of the chlorine but it does not eliminate it completely. If chlorine is suspected postpone your wine or beer making until the chlorine has disappeared, usually after a couple of days.

If the water is excessively hard it could affect the reduction of pectin in wine made from fresh fruit and it is better to boil the water, allow it to cool, and syphon it from the lime deposit. Boiling the water will disperse the free oxygen, thus denying the yeast this essential supply for their initial reproduction. The syphoned water should therefore be agitated vigorously in an open vessel to re-introduce oxygen.

5

Acid and Tannin in the Must

The skill with which you prepare the must plays a very important part in the ultimate character and life of a wine. Any error at this stage can have serious results. We have discussed in previous chapters the selection of ingredients for the type of wine you wish to make, we have talked about yeasts and sugars. When this selection has been made and you are preparing the must for fermentation, then is the time to consider the acid and tannin content. For although it is possible to adjust these components after fermentation, wines made that way never have the same quality as those made from correctly balanced musts.

Acidity

Wines produced from musts which are low in acid are flabby, un-interesting and lack bite. They are also prone to spoilage during storage by bacteria, moulds and spoilage yeasts. They very often acquire bitter, medicinal flavours (although bitterness can also be caused by other factors). The amount of acid in the wine will also influence its maturing process as the bouquet and flavour of a mature wine is brought about by the interaction of acids and alcohols.

Acidity in wine is modified by the alcohol content. A wine that is low in alcohol will taste more acid than one with a higher alcohol level. Sugar also has a masking effect on acidity. These substances, however, do not neutralise the acid. A wine with a high acid content will always have a longer life than one with a low acid content.

The acid content of the must obviously depends in the first instance on the acid content of the fruit used. The acid content of fruit can be affected by climatic conditions prevailing during ripening or by the degree of ripeness of the fruit when picked. Then there are all the different varieties of the same fruit. For example cooking apples have a higher acid content than dessert apples, and the acid content of gooseberries varies considerably with the variety. Indigenous British fruits vary in their acid content from $\frac{1}{2}$% to 3%. Musts prepared from ingredients other than fruit, such as root vegetables, flowers and grains, will certainly be deficient in acid and that from some dried fruits, such as raisins, sultanas, dates and figs, will also need adjusting.

For a beginner, a simple way of assessing the acidity of the must is by taste. When the must has been prepared and the sugar added, taste the fruit juice. It should be possible to taste the acid through the sugar. If the acid cannot be tasted it is insufficient and more should be added until the acidity can be clearly tasted. Use citric acid to adjust the acid content of the must of all fruits except grapes. For grape must use tartaric acid, since this is the prime natural acid found in grapes. $\frac{1}{4}$ oz. acid added to 1 gallon of must will increase the acidity by 1 part per thousand (p.p.t.). Since the desired acidity is usually between 3 and 4·5 parts per thousand, extra acid should be added in very small quantities at a time, so as not to over-do it.

If there is too much acid in the must, dilute it with water or with a solution of potassium carbonate. Make up a solution of 9 oz. potassium carbonate to 1 pint water; $\frac{1}{2}$ fl. oz. of this solution added to 1 gallon must or wine will reduce the acidity by 1 p.p.t.

Titration

More ambitious wine makers can check the acidity of the must accurately by titration. This is a method of neutralising the acid in a wine with an alkali of known strength. An indicator is added to the wine in order to observe the colour change that takes place when all the acid is neutralised. The alkali used is sodium hydroxide at a strength of 0·1 normal. The colour indicator is 1% phenolphthalein in methylated spirit. If a few drops of this indicator are added to the solution and the solution remains colourless, it is acid, but if the solution is slightly alkaline the colour immediately changes to pink. In practice, sodium hydroxide solution is added to the must in small amounts until the end point is reached. The amount of sodium hydroxide added is then halved and the figure achieved is equivalent to the number of parts per thousand of sulphuric acid in the must (sulphuric acid is used as a standard throughout Europe, though some wine making books express the acidity as tartaric or citric acid – see table on page 49—in fact, there is no sulphuric acid in wine).

This process is very simple and with a little practice the amateur wine maker can measure the acid content of his wine with great accuracy.

Equipment
1 10-millilitre burette graduated in millilitres (ml.)
1 10-millilitre pipette
1 250-millilitre conical flask
Decinormal solution of sodium hydroxide (0·1N)
1% solution of phenolphthalein in methylated spirit
Distilled water

Method
Using the pipette, transfer 10 ml. of the wine to be tested into the conical flask and dilute it with 20 ml. of distilled water, then add 2–3 drops of the phenolphthalein solution. Pour some of the sodium hydroxide into the burette and zero it. Place the conical flask on a sheet of white paper as this will make the colour change easier to observe.

Add sodium hydroxide a little at a time to the wine. Swirl the flask continuously and keep adding more solution until the first sign of pink colour appears. Now add the sodium hydroxide in minute amounts until the solution turns bright pink throughout. This is called the end point, and indicates that all the acid in the wine has been neutralised.

Now read from the burette how much alkali has been added. Let us assume it is 6 ml. This means that 6 ml. of 0·1N sodium hydroxide solution is required to neutralise the acid in 10 ml. of wine. If we use the equation $\dfrac{6 \times 0 \cdot 1}{10}$ the result shows an acid content of 0·06. In order to express this calculation in terms of sulphuric acid we have to multiply 0·06 by its gram equivalent weight of sulphuric acid, which is 49 gm./l. 0·06 x 49 = 2·94 gm./l., which for practical purposes may be regarded as 3 p.p.t.

As 6 ml. of 0·1N sodium hydroxide solution were used to neutralise the acid, we need only have halved it to achieve the figure of 3 p.p.t. – the acidity of the wine. So for a quick calculation, halve the amount of alkali used and call it p.p.t. sulphuric acid. For example, if 8 ml. of sodium hydroxide were added, this would indicate an acidity of 4 p.p.t.; 7 ml. would indicate an acidity of 3·5 p.p.t. This quick calculation is quite accurate enough for most amateurs.

The colour indicator naturally shows up best on white wine, but with practice it can also be used for red wine. To help you see the colour change in red wine more easily, add 40 ml. of distilled water to the wine sample; the end point will then be indicated by a bluish black colour.

It is advisable to perform two or three titrations and take the average result. Carry out titrations in daylight as artificial light makes it difficult to observe the colour changes. If you wish to test a wine that is already fermenting, boil the wine for a few minutes first to disperse the carbon dioxide; measure the wine before boiling and again when it has cooled and make up any loss with distilled water. Make sure the wine is at room temperature before testing.

The desired acidity

The acidity of dry wines is lower than that of sweet wines. As a general rule the acidity of dry wines is between 3 and 4 p.p.t. A hock type wine has a little more acid – about 4·5 p.p.t. The sweeter wines may carry anything between 3·5 and 4·5 p.p.t. If the acidity is lower than you require, increase it with citric or tartaric acid, as described on page 47. If it is higher, dilute the must with water.

Relative values

Throughout this book acidity in the wine is expressed as parts per thousand of sulphuric acid. This is because sulphuric acid is the Standard used in continental Europe. However, some winemakers

Sulphuric Acid	Citric Acid	Tartaric Acid
1·0	1·43	1·53
1·5	2·14	2·29
2·0	2·86	3·06
2·5	3·58	3·83
3·0	4·29	4·59
3·5	5·01	5·36
4·0	5·72	6·12
4·5	6·44	6·89
5·0	7·15	7·65
5·5	7·87	8·42
6·0	8·58	9·19

prefer to refer to citric or tartaric acid and it may be useful to be able to compare the relative values. The table shown on page 49 provides this comparison.

Tannin content

Tannin is essential to the balance of a wine, for without it the wine would be dull to the palate and difficult to clear. It improves the keeping qualities of a wine and ensures that it remains healthy. Tannin has bitter, astringent qualities that give an 'edge' to the wine so that wines with a high tannin content will take several years to mature, needing storage for a year in cask, followed by at least a year in bottle. Astringency in the wine decreases with age, leaving it more mellow.

Wines which lack tannin are nearly always difficult to clear and wine finings have to be used. These need the presence of tannin to work efficiently; the two substances react together, enmeshing the particles which give the haze and depositing them on the bottom of the container.

Different proportions of tannin in the must play an important part in creating wines of different types. Among commercial wines, for instance, the high tannin content of claret is one of the chief features which distinguish it from a Burgundy. Rosé wines have less astringency than red, and white have even less than rosé. This is because red wine is made by fermenting the pulp of black grapes, including skins and pips, which extracts plenty of tannin. Rosé wine is made by fermenting the pulp for a very short time, to extract small amounts of colour and tannin from the skins, and then filtering off the juice. A white wine is produced from juice only, which gives much less tannin.

Tannin is present in varying quantities in the skins and pips of fruit, in the peel of pears, in oak and walnut leaves, tea and vine prunings. The juice from grapes grown for wine usually has enough tannin of its own to make an acceptable white wine, but dessert grapes may require a small addition. Some ingredients lack tannin and in these cases additional tannin may be added. This is readily available from suppliers of wine-making equipment in liquid form, with directions for use. A cheaper alternative is to buy dried, powdered grape tannin and make up a solution yourself. A must that is low in tannin requires about 2 grams grape tannin per gallon. If using the powdered tannin, dissolve 15 g. tannin in 450 ml. boiled water; every 30 ml. (1 fl. oz.) of this solution will contain 1 g. tannin. For 1 gallon of must that is low in tannin you will therefore require 60 ml.

A wine with a high tannin content will always need 2–3 years in store to mature it. If after several years the wine is still too astringent, some of the tannin can be removed by fining with the white of an egg. Whisk one egg white with ½ pint wine, pour it gently into the bulk of the wine and stir lightly. Then rack the wine into fresh bottles. One egg white is sufficient for 5–10 gallons of wine.

6

The Fermentation

During fermentation, the yeasts will break down the sugar in the must into roughly 50% ethyl alcohol and 50% carbon dioxide gas which will escape from the wine. Fermentation has three stages.

1. The Lag Phase
2. Primary Fermentation
3. Secondary Fermentation

The lag phase

When the must is inoculated with the active yeast culture, the first stage of the fermentation starts. The yeasts utilise the free oxygen and nutrients in the must and begin to reproduce. They continue to do this until all the dissolved oxygen has been used up. This lag phase may last for 24 to 36 hours according to the ingredients used, the variety of yeast and the way the must has been prepared. During this time there are no visible signs of fermentation. This often causes concern to the beginner, who thinks the yeast culture is inactive, but in fact a great deal is happening.

Although the yeast culture contains many millions of yeast cells when it is added to the must, millions more are needed if fermentation is to be successful. The figure usually quoted is 1,000,000 cells per millilitre of must. The lag phase is the time when most of the yeast cells are produced; failure to achieve this build up of yeast can result in a delayed or incomplete fermentation since once the anaerobic fermentation starts, when alcohol is formed, yeast growth falls dramatically. It is essential that plenty of dissolved oxygen is present in the must to allow a rapid expansion of the yeast colony. It is therefore best to use water which has not been boiled. If boiled water has been used, the must should be stirred vigorously to aerate it. If you look at the must 24 hours after the yeast was added, it will have acquired a milky appearance from the rapid yeast growth.

Primary fermentation

This is also referred to as vigorous fermentation. When the yeast cells have consumed all the free oxygen, they start to form alcohol from the sugar. The appearance of bubbles of gas on the surface of the must indicates the beginning of the primary fermentation with its attendant alcohol formation. The bubbles appear slowly at first, but increase rapidly as fermentation gets under way and large quantities of gas are formed. More frothing may also occur on must prepared from fresh fruit that has not been treated with a pectin reducing enzyme (page 61). This is caused by the natural enzymes in the yeast cells completing the breakdown of pectin. This frothing lasts for only a short time.

Yeast production continues to a lesser extent in the early stages of the primary fermentation. As the carbon dioxide gas escapes and forms a barrier over the surface of the fermenting liquid, yeast production falls. Yeast cells cannot reproduce efficiently in the absence of oxygen.

Alcohol is produced rapidly during the primary fermentation and as the concentration of alcohol increases so the yeast cells start to die. Alcohol inhibits the metabolism of the yeast, so that when the gravity of the must has fallen by about thirty degrees, the fermentation begins to diminish. The fermentation is now entering its third stage.

Secondary fermentation

The rate of fermentation has now slowed considerably. If an adequate supply of nutrient and yeast food is present the rate of growth just about compensates for the loss of exhausted cells. The number of active cells therefore remains fairly constant. If on the other hand the must is lacking in yeast food then the number of yeast cells will gradually diminish until fermentation stops. If the fermentation has reached a successful conclusion, either all the fermentable sugar has been used up, or the amount of alcohol produced has overtaken the maximum alcohol tolerance of the yeast. In the first case, the wine will be dry, because a very small sugar residue will be left in the wine. In the second case there may be more sugar present giving a medium sweet or sweet wine.

If the point of alcohol tolerance has coincided with the sugar being used up, the wine will again be dry.

RELATION OF GRAVITY TO ALCOHOL CONTENT			
Gravity	Alcohol % v/v.	Gravity	Alcohol % v/v.
40 (1.040)	4.5	75 (1.075)	10.0
45 (1.045)	5.3	80 (1.080)	10.8
48 (1.048)	5.7	85 (1.085)	11.5
50 (1.050)	6.0	90 (1.090)	12.3
53 (1.053)	6.5	95 (1.095)	13.1
56 (1.056)	7.0	100 (1.100)	13.7
59 (1.059)	7.5	110 (1.110)	15.0
63 (1.063)	8.1	120 (1.120)	16.5
66 (1.066)	8.6	130 (1.130)	17.8
70 (1.070)	9.2		

Faulty fermentation

If the must is deficient in nutrient, the yeast cells may die before all the sugar has been utilised, resulting in a very sweet wine with a low alcohol content. This condition is known as a 'sticking fermentation'. This may also be caused by the yeast 'resting'. If it is resting the fermentation will re-start quite naturally and, provided the wine was effectively protected from the air, no harm will have come to it. If, however, the sticking continues, action should be taken as the wine is very susceptible at this stage to infection by spoilage bacteria.

First check the recipe to ensure that correct quantities of ingredients have been used. Temperature control during fermentation is also very important. All forms of life work best in a given temperature range; for yeast the effective range is between 60°F and 75°F. If the temperature falls below 55°F the yeast will stop working efficiently. If the temperature rises above 80°F the yeast will be destroyed by the heat.

Adding more yeast nutrient and stirring the wine vigorously to introduce oxygen may be sufficient to re-start the fermentation. It will not start immediately as conditions resembling the lag phase have been created and there has to be a period of yeast growth before fermentation can start again. It is advisable to remove some of the wine from the jar before stirring in the yeast nutrients, as there may be carbon dioxide gas dissolved in the wine and its release will cause the wine to froth. If you think excess sugar is the cause of sticking, the addition of 1–2 pints water per gallon will probably produce the desired effect. Alternatively, the addition of a yeast energiser will sometimes overcome a sticking fermentation.

If none of these remedies is effective, it will be necessary to introduce more yeast of the initial variety. Do not add the yeast directly to the wine as it may fail to establish itself in the alcoholic environment. Prepare a yeast starter in the normal way (page 40). When it is fermenting vigorously, syphon 1 pint of the sticking wine into a sterile jar and add the yeast culture; apply an airlock and stand the jar in a warm place. When this wine is fermenting, rack off another 2 pints of wine and add it to the new jar. Repeat this process until all the sticking wine has been transferred.

Syphoning will introduce oxygen into the wine and this will further assist yeast growth. By the same token, racking a wine that is still fermenting will often cause the fermentation to stick. As racking introduces oxygen into the wine, the yeasts start to reproduce again; fermentation will not re-start until this oxygen has been used up. Secondary fermentation can also occur in bottled wine if it is bottled too soon, or if oxygen gets in when the wine is racked into the bottles. This will be minimised by racking the wine efficiently before bottling (page 59). Recipes which advocate bottling wine only a few weeks after fermentation are best ignored.

Malo-lactic fermentation

Wine made from ingredients which have a high malic acid content are prone to malo-lactic fermentation. This is not true fermentation as no alcohol is produced and the organism responsible is a species of lactic acid bacteria which is able to convert the rather hard malic acid to the softer lactic acid. Dry wines which contain a lot of malic acid are often considerably improved by malo-lactic fermentation.

A small amount of carbon dioxide gas is produced during the conversion of the acids and this leads the winemaker to assume that a secondary fermentation is taking place in the bottle. Malo-lactic fermentation usually occurs during the first year of storage but can also take place in mature wines. As lactobaccilli are destroyed by sulphite, adding this to a finished wine will inhibit the bacteria. Where malo-lactic fermentation is desirable, in wine with a high malic acid content, sulphite should of course not be added.

Unfortunately lactobaccilli will also attack the sugar residue in the wine and this in turn will adversely affect its flavour. Any sweet wine showing signs of malo-lactic fermentation should be sulphited at once by adding a Campden tablet or 1 fl. oz. sulphite solution A to destroy the bacteria. As the lactobaccilli convert the stronger malic acid into the weaker lactic acid a reduction of acid in the wine results. Any wine that has undergone malo-lactic fermentation should therefore be checked for acidity and adjusted if necessary with citric acid or with tartaric acid in the case of grape wine.

Feeding the wine during fermentation

If a sweet, strong dessert wine is wanted, the alcohol content can be increased by adding small quantities (about 4 fl. oz.) of heavy syrup to each gallon of fermenting wine when the gravity has dropped to about 5 (1·005). This is repeated when the gravity has again dropped to below 5. As the alcohol content increases the gravity drop will slow down until after 1–2 weeks there is no further drop in gravity, as the yeasts are unable to assimilate any more sugar. The wine can then be racked, sweetened to taste and stored in the normal way.

Fermentation of wine made from fruit

Fruit wine can be made by one of two fermentation methods, juice fermentation or pulp fermentation.

Juice fermentation

Crush the fruit and extract the juice with a press. Add 1 fl. oz. sulphite solution A or 1 crushed Campden tablet for each gallon of juice, then gently stir the juice to disperse the sulphite. Put the juice in a cold place and leave it for 24 hours. During this time a lot of pulp particles will sink to the bottom of the jar. Rack the juice carefully into a clean jar, leaving behind the sediment. Using the hydrometer, measure the gravity of the juice (page 20), adjust the gravity to the desired level by the addition of heavy syrup. Check the acidity (page 47) and make any necessary adjustment. Add an active yeast culture, fit an airlock to the jar and leave it in a warm place (65°–70°F, 18°–21°C) to ferment. Take care not to overfill the jar for the primary fermentation otherwise the liquor will overflow as a result of released energy and a lot of wine will be lost. Juice fermentation is limited in its application because of the high acid content of our indigenous fruits. Examples where it can be used successfully are in production of wines from apples, pears and of course grape juice.

Pulp fermentation

Place the required amount of fruit into the fermentation vessel and crush it. Add pectolase, or another pectin reducing enzyme, as this will help in the extraction of the juice. Add 1 fl. oz. sulphite solution A or 1 crushed Campden tablet to the crushed fruit and stir well, then pour 1 gallon of cold water over the fruit. Cover the vessel with a piece of polythene sheeting or several thicknesses of material and tie securely to exclude as much air as possible from the must, and so prevent contamination by airborne spoilage yeasts and bacteria. Leave for 24 hours, then take a gravity reading of the must. Estimate the amount of sugar needed to reach the desired gravity. Strain about 2 pints of liquor from the vessel and bring this to the boil with the required amount of sugar. Allow it to cool to 80°F (27°C) then return the syrup to the fermentation vessel. When the must has cooled to 70°F (21°C) add the active yeast culture, again covering the vessel with a piece of stout polythene and tying it firmly. Polythene has a certain amount of transparency so you will be able to see what is going on.

There will be a short period before you can see any action on the surface

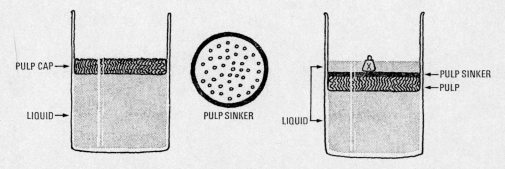

PULP CAP →   LIQUID →

PULP SINKER

LIQUID →   ← PULP SINKER   ← PULP

Use of a pulp sinker helps to prevent contamination

of the must. If a selected wine yeast is used, this period may be 24–36 hours, with granulated yeast it will be much shorter. Fermentation is in the 'lag phase'. When you see the first bubbles of carbon dioxide gas, alcoholic fermentation has started. During fermentation, particles of pulp will be raised to the surface by the bubbles of CO_2 and these will form a layer known as a 'pulp cap'. This cap is a perfect breeding ground for spoilage bacteria and it is very important that this layer is stirred into the main bulk at least twice daily. Alternatively the pulp may be kept under the surface of the liquid with a pulp sinker. This consists of a piece of wood, or inert plastic, in which $\frac{1}{4}$-in. holes have been drilled. Place this on the surface of the pulp cap, and weight it down below the surface of the liquid. Either of these methods will minimise the risk of contamination.

Ferment on the pulp for the time stated in the recipe. At the end of this time press the must, or strain it through a piece of blanket material. Material with a close warp should not be used as the cloth will be clogged very quickly. Press the pulp in the straining cloth very gently, as hard pressing will force too many pulp particles through the cloth and the wine will have to ferment on an unnecessarily heavy deposit. This is undesirable, for if fermentation is long the wine can acquire 'off' flavours from the pulp and if racked from its lees during fermentation sticking can result. Such wines can be difficult to re-ferment, particularly if the gravity has dropped to 30 or 40 (1·030 or 1·040).

After pressing or straining pour the new wine into a clean jar, fit an airlock and leave the wine in a warm place to finish fermenting.

Pulp fermentation is more widely used than juice fermentation. The time for the pulp fermentation varies according to the fruit used and the type of wine to be made. A fruit that is high in acid and tannin requires less pulp fermentation than one low in these ingredients. For instance, one can ferment the pulp of sweet cherries for up to 6 days, whereas if one fermented the pulp of elderberries for the same time the wine would be astringent. For the latter, 2 days pulp fermentation is sufficient.

Pulp fermentation is essential for red grape wine, as the red pigments in the skins of the fruit are not extracted by crushing and pressing. However, avoid excessively long periods of pulp fermentation as these tend to produce undesirable smells and flavours in the wine. Sufficient flavour and colour are extracted by fermenting the pulp for 2–6 days, depending on the fruit; 2–4 days is usually long enough.

7

Racking and Clarification

Racking

Wine must not be left in contact with its lees for any length of time or it will acquire unpleasant smells and flavours. To prevent this happening, the wine must be removed from the lees periodically and transferred to a clean, sterile jar. This process is called racking.

The easiest and most efficient way of doing this is by syphoning the wine from one container to the other using a piece of rubber or plastic tubing. Place the jar of wine on a table and the clean jar on a lower level – on a chair or the floor. Insert the inlet end of the tube into the wine until it is about 2 in. above the lees. Place the outlet end in the clean jar, at a lower level than the inlet end or the wine will not flow. In the case of the first racking after fermentation the outlet end should be high enough in the clean jar to allow the wine to splash into it; this assists dispersal of the carbon dioxide and aerates the wine, encouraging yeast growth. The yeast will be removed with the second racking, but until then it will help to clarify the wine.

Start the syphon by inserting a short piece of plastic tube into the outlet end of the main tube and sucking the tube until the wine starts to flow; pinch the tube tightly to arrest the flow, then remove the insert. Place the end of the tube in the clean jar, release the pressure and allow the wine to flow. Your mouth should not come into contact with the main tube.

As the level of the wine drops and nears the inlet end of the tube, slowly tilt the jar to keep the inlet below the surface. Now gradually lower the tube into the wine, keeping the inlet just below the surface. As soon as the suction starts to draw the lees up into the tube, draw the tube quickly out of the wine to stop the syphon. If a good sedimentary wine yeast has been used, only a few ounces of wine will be left in the jar. For the second and subsequent rackings there is no further need to

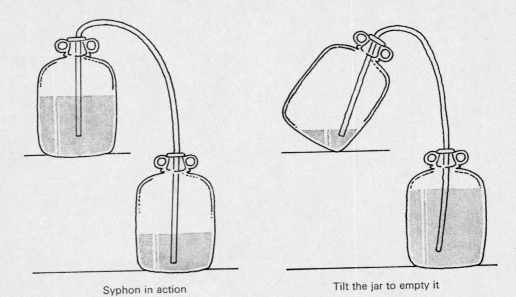

Syphon in action   Tilt the jar to empty it

aerate the wine and the outlet end of the syphon tube can be dropped right to the bottom of the jar.

It is possible to buy a more sophisticated syphon which includes a piece of glass tubing with a U-shaped end. This draws the wine from an upward position so there is less likelihood of disturbing the lees, but more wine will be left in the jar, in turn leaving a larger air space in the new container.

The wine should receive its first racking as soon as fermentation stops. The second racking should take place about 2 months later, Two more rackings at intervals of 3 months should completely clear the wine. The last three rackings should introduce as little oxygen as possible, so the outlet end of the tube should rest on the bottom of the jar to prevent splashing. The sediment in the bottom of the jar consists mainly of pulp particles, live and dead yeast cells. Racking helps to stabilise the wine by removing yeast cells, but as the first racking introduces a little oxygen there is a tendency at this stage for yeast to grow. The sediment after the first two rackings consists mainly of yeast cells.

Racking increases the possibility of over-oxidation of the wine. It is therefore common practice to add a small amount of sulphite at each racking. Use $\frac{1}{2}$–1 Campden tablet or $\frac{1}{2}$–1 fl. oz. sulphite solution A. The sulphite will also help to clear the wine.

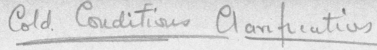
Cold Conditions Clarification

Repeated rackings will inevitably reduce the volume of the wine. The resultant air space in the storage jar should be filled wherever possible with wine of the same variety or of a similar character, or as a last resort with cold, boiled water.

Clarification

Clarification is the removal from the wine of any haze caused by pectin, starch, pulp particles, yeast, protein, metals or cream of tartar. If the must has been correctly prepared and everything has been done correctly, the wine should clear naturally; certainly a wine that does clear naturally is usually of higher quality than one which has to be filtered. Sometimes storing a new wine for a period under cold conditions will help it clear but if after 9 months in store a wine has not cleared by itself, some form of artificial clarification will be necessary.

Pectin haze

Pectin is the ingredient which jam makers look for. When present in the right proportions with sugar and acid it forms a gel and helps the jam to set. In wine, pectin is a very undesirable ingredient as it causes a haze. Since most fruits contain a certain amount of pectin, a pectin haze is a very common occurrence and there is no reason why a small amount of pectin reducing enzyme such as pectolase should not be added to the must as a matter of routine.

If the must has been prepared with cold water, sterilised with sulphite and fermented with a good wine yeast, the reduction of pectin should take place naturally. If the must has been prepared with boiling water the natural pectin reducing enzyme in the fruit, pectin methyl esterase, will have been destroyed and it is essential to add pectolase when the must has cooled. Either way, prevention is easier than cure and a small amount of pectolase can be added as a safeguard. Remember, though, that pectin reducing enzymes should not be added to a must which has a temperature in excess of 80°F.

Pectin also occurs in wine made from vegetables, particularly parsnips, where the ingredients have been boiled. If the finished wine has a haze that you suspect might be due to pectin, apply the pectin test below. After taking corrective action, be sure to rack the wine. Wine should never be left on lees that contain degraded pectin as it may acquire

an excess of methyl alcohol resulting from the breakdown of the pectin.

Pectin test

Pour 1 fl. oz. (30 ml.) wine and 3 fl. oz. (90 ml.) methylated spirit into a small bottle and shake well. The alcohol will precipitate the pectin as small globules which will later form a jelly. If the amount of pectin is small, the precipitation may be delayed for some time.

Starch

Starch haze seldom occurs except in wines made from, or incorporating, grains. If it does occur, the appropriate enzyme added to the must is again the answer. Amylozyme 100 is used to degrade starch, and full instructions are supplied by the manufacturers. Again, after the starch is degraded the wine must be racked.

Starch test

Pour about 1 fl. oz. (30 ml.) wine into a glass and add a few drops of tincture of iodine. If starch is present, the wine will assume a blue/black colour.

Pulp and yeast hazes

Given repeated racking and sufficient tannin in the must, most well made wine will clear during the first 6 months after fermentation. If after 9 months it is still not clear, and pectin or starch are not suspected, the cause is likely to be a pulp or yeast haze, and a fining agent can be used. Before using a fining agent, make sure that there is enough tannin in the wine; this is essential if the fining agent is to clear the wine successfully. Red wines usually contain enough but white wines may need a little extra; be careful not to add too much or the balance of the wine may be disturbed. Fining removes some tannin from the wine, so a fined wine may need some readjustment to restore its tannin balance. On the other hand, red wines with an excess of tannin are sometimes improved by fining.

Fining agents

A number of proprietary fining agents are available from equipment suppliers, some in handy packets sufficient for 1 gallon. Full instructions for use are given with each product.

Isinglass

One of the oldest fining agents is isinglass, an extract from the swim bladders of fish. It is seldom used nowadays as it is difficult to handle and it is never practical for use in small batches of wine.

Very little is required, $\frac{1}{2}$ oz. being sufficient for 25–30 gallons of wine; if too much is used it stays suspended in the wine. When using isinglass, grind the fibres in a mortar, then soak them overnight in a little water with a pinch of tartaric acid added. Stir the resultant jelly into 1 pint of the wine, then add it to the bulk.

Bentonite

Bentonite is a montmorillanite clay which swells in water. It is widely used in the U.S.A. and is gaining popularity in the U.K. It is simple to use and will not adversely affect the wine if too much is used. It even works efficiently in wines with low tannin content.

Never add bentonite directly to wine. Always mix it with water first and leave the solution to mature before using. Mix 1 oz. bentonite with 10 fl. oz. warm water. Add a little of the water to the bentonite and mix to a smooth paste, then add the rest of the water slowly, stirring continuously. Pour the suspension into a screw topped jar, screw on the top and shake the jar vigorously for 5–10 minutes. Leave for at least 24 hours and preferably several weeks before using.

If you are likely to need a lot of bentonite, make up two jars each containing 10 fl. oz. water and 1 oz. bentonite. When the first jar is emptied, bring the second into use and mix a fresh solution in the first jar. This way you will always have a plentiful supply of well mixed bentonite. $1\frac{1}{2}$ fl. oz. of this mixture is usually sufficient for 1 gallon wine with a light haze. For a heavy haze, use 2 fl. oz. Mix it with the wine by rolling the jar back and forth; do not stir the wine as this would introduce too much oxygen. Store the wine in a cool place for 2 weeks, then rack it and filter it if necessary.

Filtration

If your wine has a haze caused by yeast cells and pulp particles, it should be cleared by filtering. One of the quickest ways is to use a filter of asbestos pulp. However, there has been a lot of controversy about asbestos pulp as a health hazard. Continuous inhalation of the dust (such as experienced by those manufacturing it) can cause lung disease; but there is no evidence that very small amounts of asbestos in wine and beer have any harmful effect. It is for each person to decide whether or not he wishes to use it. Alternatively there are one or two sophisticated wine filters available from equipment suppliers, which are very efficient if correctly used. They have the advantage of being enclosed, minimising oxidation; also, once the filter has been started the action is continuous and the filter will run without further attention. Directions for use are given with these filters.

Asbestos pulp

If you choose to use asbestos pulp, put about 1 heaped tablespoonful into a quart jug. Add a little water and stir with a wooden spoon; add more water, stirring constantly, until the jug is full. Place a large funnel in the mouth of a jar and put a 3-in. square pad of cotton wool lightly inside the funnel, so that it covers the outlet. Place the bowl of a small wooden spoon on the cotton wool plug to prevent it from rising. Now pour the asbestos pulp mixture slowly into the funnel down the handle of the wooden spoon. The asbestos should settle over the cotton wool, forming a filter bed.

The asbestos now has to be washed to remove all traces of flavour, before the wine can be passed through it. To do this, fill up the funnel with cold water; pour in the water slowly and carefully so as not to disturb the filter bed. You will need to put at least $\frac{1}{2}$ gallon of water through the filter before all traces of asbestos taste are removed; towards the end, taste some of the filtered water and if there is any remaining flavour, continue washing.

When the filter bed is soaked with water, the first few fl. oz. of wine filtered through will be diluted; keep this fraction apart from the bulk. Pour the wine into the funnel down the handle of a wooden spoon to avoid disturbing the filter bed and keep the funnel as full as possible; the weight of the wine assists its passage through the filter. Never allow the filter pad to dry out. All the while you are filtering, keep the top of the funnel covered with a sheet of thin polythene, to exclude air and allow you to observe the wine level.

8

Cellarcraft

Many good wines are spoiled through lack of attention during storage. Wine requires as much care while it is maturing as it does during the preparation and fermentation. To rack a wine after fermentation, then put it away and forget it is asking for trouble.

Wine is usually stored in bulk during the first year of its life. During this time, if well looked after, it will clear and stabilise. Red table wines with a high astringency, or port and sherry type wines, will benefit from a further nine to twelve months in cask. When storing wines in bulk, never leave more than $\frac{1}{4}$ in. air space between the wine and the cork, and never leave the wine on its sediment for too long.

Wine may be stored in bulk in a variety of types of container, each requiring slightly different treatment.

Casks

Wooden casks are ideal containers for heavy, fortified wines and for red table wines. Some sweet white wines are also improved by a short period in a cask but the use of casks for delicate dry white wine is not recommended. As the wood of a cask is slightly porous, the wine is able to breathe a limited amount of air, and a slow process of oxidation begins. The wood also imparts some of its own flavour to the wine.

Casks must be cleaned and sterilised before use, with the exception of casks that have recently been used for spirit or fortified wine; neither of the latter will harm a dessert wine. If a cask has contained wine, fill it with boiling water with a handful of washing soda added. Leave it until the water has cooled, then empty it. Brush the inside with a stiff brush, rinse several times with fresh water and disinfect it with a sulphite solution, using 1 part sulphite solution B to 8 parts water. Fill the cask two-thirds full with this solution, fit the bung and leave it for half an hour, rolling the cask from time to time. Empty it and rinse again with cold water to remove any excess of sulphite.

Never leave a cask empty. Clean and sterilise it after use and preferably refill it straight away with new wine. If you have no new wine ready for storage, pour 1 gallon of sulphite solution, made up as above, into the cask and replace the bung. Roll the cask at least once a month to keep the whole of the wood wet and renew the sulphite solution every second month. This will keep the cask in condition ready for use at any time.

A cask that has been used for beer is likely to have a slight hop flavour remaining in the wood. This can be removed by using the cask to ferment a batch of wine, preferably grain wine since this will carry the hop flavour without too much detriment to the wine. The same cask can then be cleaned as usual and used for storage.

Storing wine in cask

Before putting wine into cask for storage, be sure it is reasonably clear, otherwise it will have to be racked at a later stage to prevent contamination by contact with the lees. Store full casks in a cradle, resting on their metal end hoops. This ensures that the ends are always wet and prevents the access of too much air to the wine.

When deciding how long to leave a wine in cask, remember that the larger the cask, the lower is the ratio of its surface area to the amount of wine, and the slower is the process of oxidation; the smaller the cask, the sooner the wine will mellow. Wine stored in a $4\frac{1}{2}$-gallon cask will require less time than wine stored in a 30-gallon cask.

Store a full cask in a cradle, resting on its metal end hoops

The wine will also evaporate slightly through the porous wood, so keep a careful watch on the air space under the bung. Except in the case of a sherry or port type wine, any loss should be made up at intervals, if possible with wine of the same variety or failing that with wine of a similar type. Wine stored under a large air space will oxidise too quickly and taste 'off', or it may become contaminated by airborne bacteria. These things are particularly likely in casks because of the porosity of the wood.

A cask that smells vinegary or mouldy should never be used as it is almost impossible to bring it back into condition.

Stone jars

Stone jars, being opaque, are ideal for bulk storage of wine. They are, however, difficult to handle if they hold more than 2 gallons. Smaller containers are much more suitable.

These should be carefully inspected before use to make certain that they are clean and free from infection. To clean, use hot water, bleach and a stiff brush, then rinse well with water. Use a torch to inspect the inside, and remove any deposit. Finally, sterilise with sulphite solution and rinse again. As with a cask, any wine stored in a stone jar should be cleared first.

Glass containers

Glass containers are ideal for early storage, as the sediment can be seen easily and this will help you decide when to rack the wine. Glass containers are available in a variety of sizes from the 1-gallon storage jars to 5-, 10-, and 15-gallon carboys. They are easily cleaned, but should be stored away from the light when filled with wine. Glass is fragile, and protection for the larger carboys is advisable.

Polythene containers

Polythene is suitable only for short periods of storage, and then should be used only if no alternative is available. The acid and alcohol in the wine may leach out some of the plasticiser from the polythene, which will adversely affect the flavour of the wine.

Bottles

All wine other than fortified wines such as sherry and port types should be bottled in punted bottles. The punt is the large 'dimple' in the base of the bottle; its purpose is to prevent any deposit that may form while the wine is in bottle from being disturbed until the last of the wine is poured.

Most wines are adversely affected by light and in almost all cases, therefore, tinted glass is used. There are certain traditional colours of glass used for different types of wine. Dry white wines are bottled in green or amber bottles, sweet white in clear glass or green tinted bottles. Red wine is stored in dark green bottles, while rosé may be stored in clear or green tinted glass. For sparkling wines, champagne-type bottles should always be used, which are dark green. Sherry and port type wines are kept in either green or amber tinted bottles, which need not be punted.

As with all other containers, bottles should be cleaned and sterilised before use. Remove any deposit clinging to the insides with a bottle brush; if the deposit from a red wine is difficult to remove, pour a little household bleach into the bottle, swirl it round and the deposit should come off easily. Then rinse the bottle thoroughly to remove all traces of bleach. Sterilise the bottles with sulphite solution B, rinse with cold boiled water and cork them loosely to exclude air.

Bottling wine

Wine to be bottled must be clear and stable. Before starting the syphon, add half a crushed Campden tablet or $\frac{1}{2}$ fl. oz. sulphite solution A to each gallon to be bottled. Syphon very carefully into the bottles, taking care not to introduce any oxygen. Fill the bottles to within $\frac{1}{2}$ in. of the cork and cork each bottle loosely to exclude air until you are ready to fix the corks permanently. To estimate how full the bottle is, hold the cork on the outside of the bottle, with the top of the cork flush with the top of the bottle. As corks vary in length it is important to check this each time.

Corks

Corks used for final bottling must be straight sided, with no flange. Never use tapered corks.

Cork in its natural state is quite hard. To soften them for use, soak the corks overnight in a solution of 1 fl. oz. sulphite solution B to 10 fl. oz.

water. Keep them submerged in this solution until you are ready to use each one, then wipe it and drive it into the bottle with a mallet and a short piece of wooden dowel, or with a corking machine. Then cover the neck of the bottle with a metal or plastic capsule (page 22) to prevent the cork being attacked by cork moth. Store filled bottles on their sides to prevent the corks from drying out. If you have no wine rack, use a partitioned carton with a piece of wood under the front edge to give it a slight tilt.

Cellar

The ideal place for storing wine is of course a cellar that stays cool and dark all the year round. But as most modern houses are built without one, an alternative storage place has to be found. The requirement is for a dark place, free from vibration and with an even temperature of about 55°F (13°C) throughout the year. A loft is not usually a good place for wine storage as too much temperature fluctuation can lead to undesirable chemical changes in the wine. A cupboard under the stairs is a much more suitable place, or if the house has a suspended wooden floor, the wine can be stored between the joists.

All wines will oxidise slightly after bottling; this is known as bottle sickness and will disappear after about a month in bottle. Leave the wine in bottle for at least six months before drinking, to further mature and improve its quality.

9

Wine Disorders

Disorders in wine are caused either by some fault in your method or by bacterial infection. Those caused by faulty methods are of course much the easiest to spot and prevent, but much can be done to prevent and to counteract bacterial infection.

Disorders caused by faulty methods

Disorder	Cause	Remedy
Bitterness in the finished wine	Lack of acid in the must	See page 47
	Excess tannin in the must	See page 51
	Wild yeasts	See Bacterial Infection, below
	The inclusion in the must of bitter ingredients such as the pith of citrus fruits	More careful preparation of ingredients
Lees odour or flavour	Leaving the wine too long on its lees	More frequent racking
Mustiness	Dirty or stale equipment and storage vessels	Sterilisation of all equipment immediately before use
Excessive oxidation	Inefficient racking	Be sure outlet end of syphon is on the bottom of the jar
	Too large an air space in storage containers	Topping up
Unpleasant smells and flavours	Too long a period of fermentation	More careful timing

Bacterial infection

The air around us contains many living organisms that are enemies to wine. This is particularly true of air around rotting fruit or fermenting matter. Such is the power of these organisms that they will, if ignored, completely break down the wine until it becomes no more than water with a little carbonic acid gas and some sludge in the bottom of the jar.

Acetification

An acetified wine will taste and smell very strongly of vinegar. This is most frequently caused by the presence of the organism mycoderma aceti (acetobacter); this transforms the alcohol into acetic acid by oxidation. Alternatively it may be caused by leaving the wine exposed to air, or by the use of contaminated equipment.

Acetification generally occurs in the must before the anaerobic fermentation, or in a young wine with a low alcohol content. It may also occur in an unbalanced wine if excessive air space is left in the storage container. If contamination is detected very early during fermentation it is sometimes possible to save the wine by sulphiting it heavily with 3 Campden tablets or with 2 fl. oz. sulphite solution A. After adding the sulphite leave it for 2 days then start the fermentation again, using a fresh yeast culture. Much of the acetic acid will be removed by this second fermentation, but some will remain and the finished wine is rarely worth the extra work involved. If a finished wine becomes contaminated, it is best to put it aside to allow acetification to run its full course and produce wine vinegar for kitchen use. Alternatively, pour it away, taking care to do this well away from the winery. Sterilise all contaminated equipment with sulphite solution B to prevent contamination of the next batch of wine.

To prevent acetification:
1. Sterilise all equipment, especially fermentation vessels and storage jars, before and after use.
2. Sterilise all ingredients used in the must.
3. Keep containers well covered during fermentation.
4. Use a pulp sinker (page 57), or stir the must frequently when fermenting on the pulp.
5. Always keep an airlock in position during fermentation in the jar,

and make sure there is an effective seal between airlock and cork and between cork and the mouth of the jar.

6. Avoid excessive airspace in storage containers.
7. Make sure that fruit flies cannot get at must or wine.
8. Ensure that the wine reaches an alcohol content of at least 11% v/v (page 84).

Flowers of wine

This is a whitish grey film that forms on the surface of the wine. It is caused by mycoderma, or film yeasts. These organisms form whitish grey flecks on the surface of the wine, which multiply to form small patches and ultimately cover the whole surface. If the film is disturbed it may sink to the bottom, but will reform later. The organism acts by attacking the alcohol in the wine and converting it into carbon dioxide and water. The carbon dioxide gas collects in small pockets under the film, giving it an undulating appearance. It also attacks the flavour, so that the wine becomes flat and insipid.

Flowers of wine usually appear on wine that is stored with too much air space in the container and particularly affects poor wines with a low alcohol content. If the disorder is discovered early, the wine can be saved by filling the container with more wine so that it overflows, taking the film with it. Then sulphite the wine with 2 Campden tablets or 2 fl. oz. sulphite solution A. Leave the wine for 24 hours and then rack into a sterile container. Sterilise all equipment that has been exposed to the infection with sulphite solution B, or a solution of 6 Campden tablets dissolved in 1 pint water.

To prevent flowers of wine developing, adopt the measures listed for prevention of acetification (above).

Ropiness or oiliness

When affected by this disorder, the wine assumes a thick, oily consistency and pours like heavy oil. Although the flavour is not unduly affected, its appearance makes the wine undrinkable. Ropiness is caused by a species of lactic acid bacteria which usually affects white wines with a low alcohol content. It will not occur in a wine with an alcohol content of 13% v/v or more. The remedy is to kill the bacteria by adding 2 Campden tablets or 1 fl. oz. sulphite solution A to the wine. Stir the sulphite into the wine vigorously until it assumes a normal appearance, then let it stand for 2 days before racking into a sterile jar. Filtering may also be necessary.

A wine that has been treated like this will have a short life. Allow a month for it to recover from its rough treatment, then drink it.

Metallic disorders

If the wine has been in contact with iron, brass, copper, lead, zinc or other poisonous metals it may acquire a haze, darken and have an unpleasant flavour. If this happens, discard it as it may be injurious to health.

10

Grapes and Grape Wine

There is evidence that in the past grapes were grown extensively in the southern part of England, Gloucestershire, Hertfordshire and the Cotswolds. Now, in the twentieth century, we have a great revival of grape growing. Once again sizeable vineyards are being laid down, wine from them is produced commercially and a great deal of research has been carried out in propagating and selecting varieties of grape vines best suited to our climate. A good selection of vines is available to the amateur who wishes to grow his own grapes in the garden or on a wall of his house.

Growing your own grapes

Vines are very adaptable and they grow in almost any soil, provided it is well drained. However, take care when choosing the variety; some vines do better under certain soil conditions and vines which grow well under glass do not always fruit well outdoors. It is best to consult the nurseryman from whom you are going to make your purchase. Describe your garden aspect and soil conditions and he will advise you on the variety of vine to plant. Generally speaking, white varieties ripen better outside than red.

Planting and pruning

First decide where you want to plant the vine. Remember once the vine is planted it will be there for a long time. If planted near a wall it will grow and cover a sizeable area. The root structure of an established vine is very large, extending over a considerable area from the main root stock and the roots themselves penetrate to a great depth. The best time to plant vines outside is from October to mid November; they can also be planted in the spring.

Next prepare the soil. Remember that good drainage is essential. Dig a hole 2 ft. 6 in. deep, and wide enough to accommodate the **root** structure without restriction. The bottom of the hole should have a 6 in. layer of broken brick rubble; over this place a layer of turf, grass side undermost, then fill the hole with a mixture of loam, rotted leaves and a little wood ash from the garden bonfire. Disentangle the roots of the young vine by putting them in a pail of water, remove enough soil from the hole to take this root structure, then put the vine into the hole and spread the roots evenly. By hand, work some sifted soil between the roots until they are all covered, then firm the roots down by treading. Fill the hole with the loam mixture. Water the vine in well and cover the soil around it with a layer of manure to conserve moisture.

CORDON AND ESPALIER VINES
If the vine is grown on a wall of the house it can be trained as a cordon or an espalier. Prune the young vine above a bud about 20 in. from the soil. Allow the three top buds to grow, but rub off all buds below these when they break. Train the centre bud vertically, the other two horizontally, one to the left, the other to the right. The following winter prune the shoots back to about half their length. When growth starts the horizontal shoots will produce side shoots; rub off all shoots on the underside of the horizontal canes and limit those on the upper side to one shoot per foot. Rub off shoots on the vertical cane that are not required for further horizontal shoots and train the top shoot on the vertical cane upwards. Repeat this procedure yearly until all the available wall space is covered. Cutting the canes back ensures sturdy growth.

THE GUYOT SYSTEM
Vines which are grown without the support of a wall require different treatment. A very effective method of pruning is the Guyot system. After planting, cut back the vine to two buds and grow on these two shoots for the first season. The following January select and retain the stronger cane and cut back the weaker one to two buds. Cut back the strong cane to seven or eight buds and tie it to a supporting wire; this will be the fruiting cane.

   The vine should not be allowed to carry fruit until it is four years old, and then only one or two bunches for the first year. The two buds from the weaker spur will produce canes; tie these loosely to a stake. The following January remove the fruiting cane, select the stronger of the two canes produced during the season, cut it back to seven or eight buds and tie it to the lowest supporting wire; the weaker cane is again cut back to two buds. This system can be continued for many years and requires a minimum of pruning.

If you are growing more than one vine it is advisable to erect a supporting system of stakes and wires. Plant the vines 4 ft. apart in rows running from north to south. Place a strong post firmly at the end of each row and brace it to avoid wire slackening. A long row will of course require more than two stakes. Fix wires between the stakes, the first one about 15 in. from ground level and the other two at about 16-in. intervals above the first. Further support can be given to the season's growth of replacement canes by placing a heavy bamboo cane at each station. Tie the canes loosely to the stake.

In addition to the winter pruning, it is necessary to restrict leaf growth in spring and early summer. This is done by disbudding un-productive growth. All side shoots growing from the leaf axils should be pinched out; fruiting canes should be stopped two leaves from the flower cluster; non fruiting canes should be stopped at the sixth leaf. Replace-ment canes should all have the axil shoots removed and should be shortened to 5 ft. in August to help the wood to ripen.

Basal spring growths should be pinched out or broken off. While it is perfectly safe to prune soft growth, seasoned wood should never be pruned during the growing season. If a seasoned cane is inadvertently cut seal it with a special compound obtained from a horticultural shop, otherwise the vine will 'bleed'. Check from time to time to ensure that the wire supports have not slackened. The vines make considerable growth during a season and can easily be damaged by strong winds if not adequately supported.

Fertiliser

If the soil around the vine is lacking in humus, apply a light dressing of farmyard or hop manure every third year, spreading it well around the vine. When the grapes have formed, weak liquid manure can be given; a light dressing of an inorganic fertiliser may be given in alternate years.

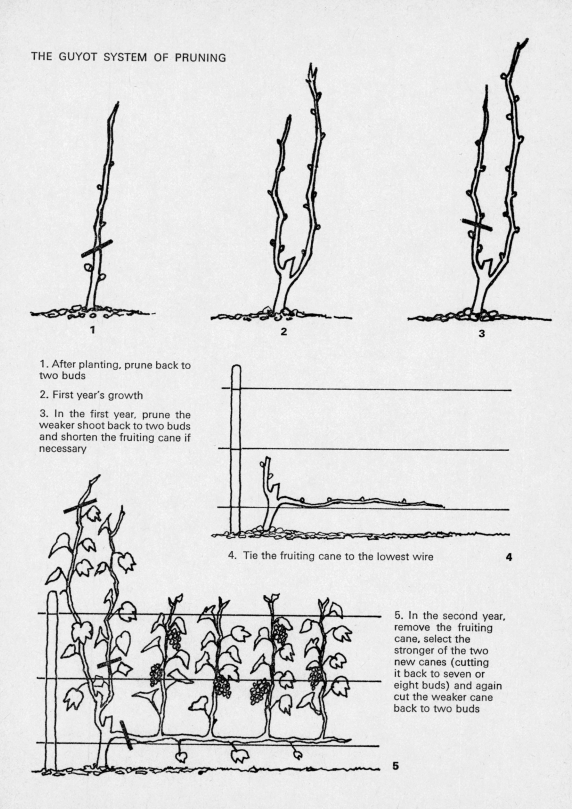

THE GUYOT SYSTEM OF PRUNING

1. After planting, prune back to two buds

2. First year's growth

3. In the first year, prune the weaker shoot back to two buds and shorten the fruiting cane if necessary

4. Tie the fruiting cane to the lowest wire

5. In the second year, remove the fruiting cane, select the stronger of the two new canes (cutting it back to seven or eight buds) and again cut the weaker cane back to two buds

Vine disorders

Powdery mildew
Powdery mildew appears as a powdery white growth on the stems, leaves and fruit. The danger period is June and July. Once the disease appears, it spreads very rapidly and unless checked will ruin the fruit crop; a lot of grapes will fall off and those remaining will not develop properly, but will crack and dry off. The most effective remedy is sulphur. This may be applied either as dust or spray. Mildew fungicides are available and should be applied as directed by the manufacturers. Some of the modern hybrid grapes are claimed to be resistant to mildew, but it is better to spray, as a precaution, just before the flowers open.

Downy mildew
This disease is closely related to potato blight, and thrives in wet, humid conditions. The first sign is the appearance of small greenish yellow spots on the leaves of the vine and a whitish mould on the underside of the leaves. The disease will eventually attack all parts of the vine. Downy mildew is readily controlled by immediate spraying with Bordeaux mixture.

Vine propagation
Grape vines are easily propagated from January prunings. Choose canes that have previously borne fruit. The shoots should be about 9 in. long and have at least three buds. Tie these lengths in small bundles and store in damp sand in a frost-free place until March. No elaborate preparation of the soil is necessary before planting; just push a spade into the soil to make a narrow slit, push the shoot into this slit until the top bud is just above ground, then firm the soil around the cutting to help root growth. If you use this method, unnecessary loosening of the soil is prevented. Vines can also be propagated by buds but as this method involves a propagating frame in a warm greenhouse, with a bottom heat of about 75°F, the cutting method is more practical for the amateur.

A vine should have a good healthy leaf structure, as the sugar content of the grapes is greatly influenced by the leaves of the vine. In Britain we are at a climatic disadvantage. In warmer regions with plenty of sunshine, during ripening the acid in the fruit decreases as the sugar increases. With low sunshine, anything that can be done to assist ripening of the fruit needs careful consideration. Planting the vine against a wall to obtain reflected heat, choosing the sunniest position in the garden, pruning to help the wood to ripen and tying the fruiting canes near to the ground all help to ripen the fruit. Ripe grapes are a big attraction to birds and ripening bunches have to be protected with netting. If wasps cause damage to ripe grapes, the best method of defence is to search out the nest and destroy it.

Grape wine

Grapes which are grown for wine should be as ripe as possible when they are gathered. In a wet and cold season it is very likely that the grapes will have a high acid and low sugar content. It will then be necessary to add sugar and reduce the acidity. The main acids contained in grape juice are tartaric and malic acids and the amounts will vary according to the season.

The extra sugar is made up into heavy syrup and added to the juice. This will also slightly reduce acidity by dilution; however, if the acidity is still too high, it may be further reduced by adding potassium carbonate as described on page 47; $\frac{1}{2}$ fl. oz. of this solution per gallon of must will reduce the acidity by 1 p.p.t. The wine will also lose some of its tartaric acid during fermentation and in all probability some of it will be precipitated as cream of tartar during early storage. To assist this, store the finished wine for a period under very cold conditions. The malic acid content may also be reduced during storage by a malo-lactic fermentation. If the acidity is high, malo-lactic fermentation should be encouraged. No sulphite should therefore be added to the wine once fermentation has finished, as the bacteria responsible for the malo-lactic fermentation are susceptible to sulphite.

WHITE WINE

White wine can be made from the juice of either red or white grapes. As the stalks of the grapes contain a lot of tannin and their inclusion would result in excessive astringency, it is necessary to pick the grapes from the stalks. Then crush the grapes and press the pulp to extract the juice.

Sulphite the juice immediately with 1 Campden tablet or 1 fl. oz. sulphite solution A per gallon.

RED WINE

Red wine is made by fermenting the pulp and skins of red grapes, for a short period. The alcohol formed during this period will leach the colour from the skins.

ROSE WINE

Rosé wine is again fermented on the pulp and skins of red grapes. In this case the pulp is pressed when sufficient colour has been extracted.

Preparing the must

The preparation is the same for all three types of wine and the variations are produced by different fermentation methods. Remove the grapes from the stalks, discarding bad or mouldy grapes. The grapes have now to be crushed. This is done by passing them through a roller crusher, or coarse mincer. Alternatively, small quantities of grapes can be crushed with a wooden stave or the base of a flat bottomed bottle, using a polythene bucket as a container. Do not crush fruit in an earthenware container, as it would not be strong enough to withstand the pressure. Avoid crushing the pips as these give the wine a bitter flavour. Next, press the pulp and sulphite the juice with 1 crushed Campden tablet or 1 fl. oz. sulphite solution A to each gallon and leave for 24 hours. The sulphite will disinfect the juice and also prevent oxidation. During this time, pulp particles will sink to the bottom, leaving the juice fairly clear. Syphon this clear juice into a clean jar, leaving the pulp behind. Although this appears to be rather wasteful, the resulting wine will be better; the residue will be used later. Test the gravity of the juice with a hydrometer and adjust the sugar content where necessary. 1 lb. sugar per gallon will increase the gravity by about 32 (1·032). If a dry wine is intended the starting gravity should be between 80 and 85 (1·080–1·085). For a sweet wine the starting gravity can be increased to 100 (1·100) and the wine fed when the gravity has dropped to 5 (1·005) if a high alcohol content is required.

Check and adjust the acidity where necessary. A dry wine should have

6 Roses for wine should be delicately scented varieties.

7 Kingston Black apples for cider or wine making.

8 Titration: add sodium hydroxide to the wine solution until the pink colour indicates that the acid is completely neutralised.

an acidity of 3·5 p.p.t. and a sweet from 4·0 to 4·5 p.p.t. (both expressed as sulphuric acid).

The grapes from which the juice has been pressed will still contain a lot of goodness, and a worthwhile second run can be made. Using the lees left in the first jar as a base, make up to 1 gallon with cold water and pour this over the pulp. Add 2 tsps. pectolase, or another pectin reducing enzyme, 2 Campden tablets or 1 fl. oz. sulphite solution A and stir well. Cover closely and leave it for 24 hours. Stir well again and strain off 1½ pints of this juice. Take a gravity reading and estimate the amount of sugar required to give the starting gravity of 85. Heat the strained juice and dissolve the sugar in it. Allow it to cool to 80°F (26°C), then pour over the pulp. Stir well. Now check the acidity. The juice should have a sharp acid taste, coming clearly through the sugar. Titration would of course be more accurate to determine the acid content. Add tartaric acid, if necessary, in small amounts. Having adjusted gravity and acidity, add some yeast nutrient and an active yeast culture, cover closely and stand in a warm place. Ferment on the pulp for 3–4 days, stirring twice daily. After this, press the liquor, pour it into a jar, fit an airlock and leave in a warm place until fermentation stops.

The volume of juice in the grapes will vary slightly; 20–22 lb. grapes will usually yield 1 gallon of juice. Although this quantity of grapes appears a little expensive, when one considers that the output is 1 gallon (six bottles) of full bodied wine made from the pure juice and 1 gallon of wine made from the second run, the proposition is an economical one. If red grapes are used the output is 1 gallon of white wine and 1 gallon of red. The second run wine will obviously lack the body and quality of the first, nevertheless it will make a reasonable table wine similar to a cheap commercial blend.

Red wine
Red wine production requires a different method. The grapes are prepared and crushed as for a white wine, but the pulp is not pressed. Instead, the pulp is put into a fermentation vessel, together with 2 tsps. pectolase and 2 crushed Campden tablets or 1 fl. oz. sulphite solution A per gallon.

The vessel is covered and left for 24 hours. It is advisable to strain some of the juice and take a gravity reading. Adjust the sugar content to give a starting gravity of 90 (1·090). Test the acidity and adjust if necessary. Add an active yeast culture, cover closely and stand in warm place. Watch for the first visible signs of fermentation and when the pulp starts to rise, stir twice daily. Ferment on the pulp until sufficient colour has been extracted (4–5 days) then press. Put the juice into a jar, fit an airlock and leave in a warm place to finish fermenting. The pulp is discarded – it makes a good garden compost.

Rosé wine

Rosé wine is made by following the same procedure as red wine, but the period of pulp fermentation is shorter as less colour is required. The pulp is pressed when enough colour has been extracted, usually after 2–3 days. A temporary loss of colour may be observed initially after sulphiting but the colour will return as the sulphite disperses during fermentation.

Sweet wines

Sweet wines are made by the same method but the initial gravity is raised to 100 (1·100). If a high alcohol content is wanted, the wine is fed when the gravity has dropped to 5 (1·005). The final sugar adjustment is made at the end of fermentation.

Maturation

Grape wine requires maturing for 2–3 years before drinking. The wine can of course be drunk much earlier but might be harsh and unpalatable. White wines generally mature more quickly than red, though the length of time required for a white wine to mellow will depend to a large extent on its acid content. Red wines take longer to mature owing to their tannin content; the more astringent the wine, the longer it will take to mellow. Rosé wines are usually more palatable if they are not made too dry.

11

Wine Recipes

This chapter deals with recipes for wines made from fresh and dried fruits, flowers, herbs, grains and vegetables. It is by no means a comprehensive selection of all possible wines – this might also include wines made from mushrooms, onions, geranium leaf, lilac flower, lily of the valley flowers, Christmas pudding, Christmas cake, kohl rabi, spinach and lettuce. All have been used at some time. But effort, time and money are required to produce a gallon of wine and there is a long period of waiting before the wine is ready for drinking. It is therefore only common sense to use ingredients which will ensure a good end product. For this reason experimental recipes have not been included.

As all fruits and flowers have their own special flavour and bouquet, it seems a pity to mask this delightful natural quality by adding other flavouring ingredients. Grape concentrate is the exception. The reader can adjust any of the following recipes to include grape concentrate; however, remember that the amount of sugar needs to be adjusted as $\frac{1}{2}$ pint grape concentrate is the equivalent of $\frac{1}{2}$ lb. sugar.

How to use these recipes

Adding sugar to the must

Some wine makers add the sugar to the must in two or three stages. This is not necessary for a dry wine, provided that the initial gravity does not exceed 100 (1·100). When making sweet wines, it is better to add extra sugar in the form of heavy syrup, when the gravity has fallen to about 5 (1·005), than to dissolve it all initially. Use about 4 fl. oz. heavy syrup at a time. (Heavy syrup is made by dissolving 1 lb. sugar in $\frac{1}{2}$ pint boiling water.)

As some wines will ferment more sugar than others, specific amounts of sugar are not given in the various sweet wine recipes – the amounts given are guide lines only. The amount of sugar to be used initially

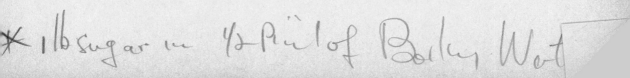

1 lb sugar in ½ Pint of Boiling Wort

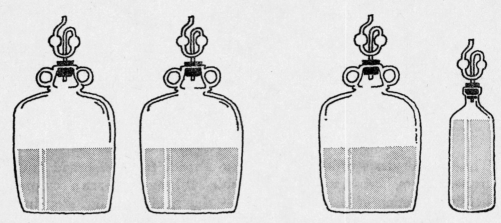

Divide the must between two jars for the vigorous fermentation, to prevent it spilling over

should not produce a gravity in excess of 100 (1·100). If this sugar is used by the yeast during fermentation, it will give an alcohol content of not less than 13% v/v. Any additional sugar added and used by the yeasts will raise the alcohol content accordingly. The last addition, not used by the yeasts, will determine the residual sugar content in the wine. If more than 3 lb. sugar is added initially, the chances are that there will not be an efficient fermentation, resulting in an oversweet, low alcohol wine resembling a cordial. It is preferable to add the sugar TO 1 gallon of water, rather than to include the sugar IN 1 gallon. In this way the volume of liquid will be increased to fill the storage jar. When making sugar adjustments 8 oz. sugar added to 1 gallon juice will increase the gravity by approximately 16 (1·016), and the volume will be increased by about 4 fl. oz.

Period of fermentation

If the recipe states '3 days pulp fermentation', this means 3 days from the day when the first visible signs of fermentation appear, not from the day when the yeast culture is added to the must. The lag phase may last 24–36 hours, so the time for straining the pulp may be 4–5 days after adding the yeast culture to the must.

General

In order to avoid repetition, where a recipe states 'The wine can be fed with sugar syrup', the procedure described on page 56 should be followed.

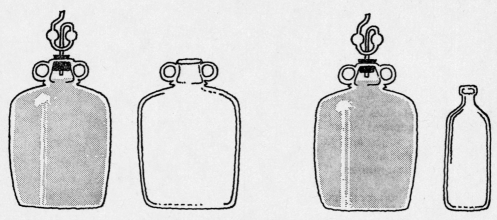

When the first fermentation subsides the must can be poured back into one jar

'Divide into two jars' means that after the addition of the yeast culture, the must is fermented in two jars until the vigorous fermentation has subsided, usually after 4–5 days. The must is then united into one jar, the airlock is re-fitted and the wine left to complete fermentation. This method prevents the wine from surging out of the jar, losing a lot of wine and attracting spoilage organisms to the area.

If the finished wine is too dry, it can be sweetened any time by the addition of heavy syrup. This should be done shortly before use but only sweeten sufficient wine for the occasion, as the addition of sugar could start fermentation if the wine is stored after sweetening.

Fruit wines

APPLES

Dessert Apples such as Cox's Orange Pippin, Merton Worcester, Cherry Cox, Sunset or Laxton's Fortune can be used successfully provided they are used straight from the tree. The chemical content of the fruit changes during storage. If stored apples are used, put a few cooking apples with them.

Green cooking apples will make a hard and acidulous wine. Some varieties of crab apples make a good wine, others give a wine that is thin and astringent. The only way to find the potential of the fruit is by trial and error.

Gathered apples will not require cleaning, but if they are picked up from the ground they should be washed under running water and any blemished parts cut away.

APPLE WINE

5 pt. (2·9 l. approx.) fresh apple juice
1½ Campden tablets or 1½ fl. oz. sulphite solution A
3 pt. (1·7 l. approx.) water
2 lb. (900 g.) sugar, approx.
1 level tsp. citric acid
1 level tsp. yeast nutrient
Chablis yeast
heavy sugar syrup, optional

Crush the apples, using a mincer with a plate which has ¼-in. holes and press the juice into a jar containing a crushed Campden tablet or 1 fl. oz. sulphite solution. This serves the dual purpose of sterilising the juice and preventing oxidation. Leave the juice in a cool place for 24 hours. During this time a lot of pulp will settle to the bottom of the jar. Rack the juice into a clean jar, leaving the sediment behind. At this stage there should be 5 pt. juice.

Heat 3 pt. water and in it dissolve the sugar, acid and yeast nutrient. Allow this to cool to 80°F (27°C) and mix it into the apple juice. Add the active yeast culture, stir well and divide the must between two jars. Fit airlocks and stand them in a warm place, at 70°F (21°C) to ferment.

When the first vigorous fermentation subsides, fill one jar gently from the other, re-fit the airlock and leave to ferment in a temperature reduced to 65°F (18°C), to slow down the fermentation. Pour any surplus must into a bottle and plug the neck with cotton wool. When fermentation is complete, rack the wine into a clean jar, add half a crushed Campden tablet or ½ fl. oz. sulphite solution A and store in a cool place.

Note : The amount of sugar given can be only approximate as the sugar content of the apples is likely to vary. To assess more accurately the amount required, mix the apple juice with the water and take a gravity reading with the hydrometer. Then use the Pearson Square (page 44) to assess the correct amount of sugar. For a dry wine, the starting gravity should be 85 (1·085) and for a sweet wine 100 (1·100). Feed a sweet wine with heavy syrup when the gravity falls to 5 (1·005).

APRICOTS

Fresh apricots are very suitable for the production of a dry table wine.

Like all stone fruit, apricots contain a high proportion of pectin and it is therefore advisable to add a pectin reducing enzyme.

APRICOT WINE (Dry)

1 lb. (450 g.) fresh apricots or ½ lb. (225 g.) dried apricots, soaked overnight and
    cooked until soft
1 gal. (4·5 l.) water
2 tsps. pectolase
1 Campden tablet or 1 fl. oz. sulphite solution A
2½ lb. (1·2 kg.) sugar
1 level tsp. yeast nutrient
all purpose yeast

Peel the fruit and remove the stones, if fresh, then chop it. Put it in a container with 6 pt. cold water, the pectolase and 1 Campden tablet or 1 fl. oz. sulphite solution A. Leave for 24 hours.

Heat 2 pt. water and dissolve in it the sugar and yeast nutrient. Allow the temperature of the mixture to fall to 80°F (27°C) and add it to the apricot must. Add the active yeast culture, cover closely and ferment the pulp for 3 days, stirring twice daily. Press the pulp and fill the juice into a 1-gal. jar. Fit an airlock and leave to ferment in a temperature of 65°F (18°C). When the wine has fermented to dryness, rack and store in a cool place.

APRICOT WINE (Sweet)

2 lb. (900 g.) fresh apricots or ¾ lb. (338 g.) dried apricots, soaked overnight and
    cooked until soft
1 gal. (4·5 l.) water
2 tsps. pectolase
1 Campden tablet or 1 fl. oz. sulphite solution A
3½ lb. (1·4 kg. approx.) sugar
1 level tsp. yeast nutrient
all purpose yeast

Make as for Apricot Wine (Dry), above, adding 3 lb. sugar initially and the remaining ½ lb. after pressing the pulp.

BILBERRIES

This is a popular fruit for making dry table wine. A wine made from the fresh fruit will be much better than wine made from dried fruit; dried bilberries can easily impart a caramel or oxidised taste to the wine. Bottled bilberries may be used in place of fresh.

Bilberries have a strong flavour; do not use too many or the flavour of the wine may be overpowering.

BILBERRY WINE (Dry)

1½ lb. (625 g.) fresh bilberries or 5 oz. (140 g.) dried bilberries
1 tsp. pectolase
1 gal. (4·5 l.) water
1 Campden tablet or 1 fl. oz. sulphite solution A
2¼ lb. (1 kg.) sugar
1 level tsp. yeast nutrient
½ pt. (284 ml.) red grape concentrate
Pommard yeast

If using dried bilberries, put them in a pan with 2 pt. of the measured water, bring to the boil and simmer for 5 minutes. Add a further 4 pt. water. Strain the pulp, put the concentrate into a fermentation vessel and add the pectolase. Then continue as for fresh fruit.

Put the fresh fruit into a fermentation vessel, crush it and add the pectolase. Add 6 pt. cold water and the Campden tablet or sulphite solution. Leave for 24 hours.

Heat 2 pt. water and in it dissolve the sugar, yeast nutrient and grape concentrate; allow to cool to 80°F (27°C) and add it to the bilberries. Next incorporate an active yeast culture, stir well, cover the vessel and ferment the pulp for 2 days, stirring twice daily. Press the pulp and strain the juice into a clean jar, fit an airlock and ferment in a warm place at 65°F (18°C) until the wine is dry. Rack and store in a cool place.

BILBERRY WINE (Sweet)

2 lb. (900 g.) fresh bilberries or ¾ lb. (338 g.) dried bilberries
1 tsp. pectolase
7 pt. (4 l.) water
1 Campden tablet or 1 fl. oz. sulphite solution A
3 lb. (1·4 kg.) sugar
1 level tsp. yeast nutrient
½ pt. (280 ml.) red grape concentrate
Pommard yeast
heavy sugar syrup, optional

Make as for Bilberry Wine (Dry), page 88, adding 5 pt. water initially instead of 6 pt. Add 2½ lb. sugar initially and ½ lb. after pressing the pulp. The wine may be fed with heavy sugar syrup when the gravity has dropped to 5 (1·005).

BLACKBERRIES

The blackberry is one of the best fruits for winemaking. It is a versatile ingredient and can be used with equal success for dry, sweet or port type wines. Cultivated blackberries have a slightly different flavour from wild berries and a slightly higher acid content. The skins of both the cultivated and wild berries contain a large amount of tannin and too much fruit will make the wine unpleasantly astringent. There is a tendency amongst amateur winemakers to use too much fruit if it is easily and cheaply obtainable; avoid this, as more often than not a wine made with too much fruit will be unbalanced. Fermenting blackberry pulp for too long will give the wine a woody flavour, derived from the pips.

BLACKBERRY WINE (Dry)

2½ lb. (1·2 kg.) ripe blackberries
1 tsp. pectolase
1 gal. (4·5 l.) water
1 Campden tablet or 1 fl. oz. sulphite solution A
3 lb. (1·4 kg.) sugar
1 level tsp. yeast nutrient
Pommard yeast
citric acid, optional

Put the fruit into a fermentation vessel and crush it. Add the pectolase, 6 pt. cold water and 1 crushed Campden tablet or the sulphite solution. Stir well, cover the vessel closely and leave for 24 hours.

Heat 2 pt. water and in it dissolve the sugar and yeast nutrient; allow to cool to 80°F (27°C), then add to the blackberries. Add an active yeast culture, stir and ferment the pulp for 3 days. Press the pulp then strain the juice into a clean 1-gal. jar, fit an airlock and ferment at 65°F (18°C) to dryness.

If the season has been dry and sunny, the must should be tested for acidity. If necessary adjust with citric acid.

BLACKBERRY WINE (Sweet)

4 lb. (1·9 kg.) blackberries
1 tsp. pectolase
1 gal. (4·5 l.) water
1 Campden tablet or 1 fl. oz. sulphite solution A
3½ lb. (1·6 kg.) sugar
1 level tsp. yeast nutrient
port yeast
heavy sugar syrup, optiona

Make as for Blackberry Wine (Dry), page 89, but add only 3 lb. sugar initially and add ½ lb. after pressing the pulp. The wine may be fed with sugar syrup when the gravity has dropped to 5 (1·005).

BULLACES

The bullace is a very old variety of stone fruit, very similar in shape to a small greengage. Yellow damsons are often mistaken for bullaces. The fruit contains a large amount of pectin, has a rather robust flavour and is better suited to a sweet wine than to a dry.

BULLACE WINE (Sweet)

3 lb. (1·4 kg.) bullaces
2 tsps. pectolase
1 gal. (4·5 l.) water
1 Campden tablet or 1 fl. oz. sulphite solution A
3½ lb. (1·6 kg.) sugar
1 level tsp. yeast nutrient
all purpose yeast
heavy sugar syrup, optional

Put the fruit into a fermentation vessel, bruise it but be careful not to break the stones. Add the pectolase and 6 pt. cold water, then add the Campden tablet (crushed) or sulphite solution A; cover the vessel and leave for 24 hours.

After this interval heat 2 pt. water and in it dissolve 3 lb. sugar and the yeast nutrient. Allow to cool to 80°F (27°C) then add to the bullaces. Add an active yeast culture, stir, cover closely and ferment on the pulp for 24 hours. Then, with well scrubbed hands, remove as many stones as possible. Ferment the pulp for another 2 days, stirring twice daily. Press the pulp, strain the juice and dissolve in it the remaining ½ lb. sugar. Pour it into a clean 1-gal. jar, fit an airlock and ferment at 65°F (18°C).

This wine may be fed with heavy sugar syrup when the gravity falls to 5 (1·005).

CHERRIES

Both dry and sweet wine can be made from cherries. Morello cherries make the best wine, but black dessert cherries also produce very acceptable wine. Dessert cherries are low in acid and the addition of a little citric acid is therefore necessary. Morello cherries have sufficient acid and do not need any adjustment. All fruit should be as ripe as possible.

MORELLO CHERRY WINE (Dry)

2½ lb. (1·2 kg.) ripe Morello cherries
2 tsps. pectolase
1 gal. (4·5 l.) water
1 Campden tablet or 1 fl. oz. sulphite solution A
2¾ lb. (1·3 kg.) sugar
1 level tsp. yeast nutrient
Pommard yeast

Put the cherries into a fermentation vessel and bruise them, taking care not to break the stones. Add the pectolase, 6 pt. cold water and a crushed Campden tablet or the sulphite solution. Cover the vessel closely and leave for 24 hours.

Heat 2 pt. water and dissolve in it the sugar and yeast nutrient, cool it to 80°F (27°C) and stir into the cherries. Add an active yeast culture, cover the vessel and ferment the pulp for 2 days at a temperature of 70°F (21°C).

With well scrubbed hands, remove as many stones as possible then ferment the pulp for a further 2 days, stirring twice daily. Press the pulp, strain the juice into a clean 1-gal. jar, fit an airlock and ferment at a temperature of 65°F (18°C), until dry. Rack into a clean jar and store in a cool place.

MORELLO CHERRY WINE (Sweet)

3½ lb. (1·6 kg.) ripe Morello cherries
2 tsps. pectolase
1 gal. (4·5 l.) water
1 Campden tablet or 1 fl. oz. sulphite solution A
3½ lb. (1·6 kg.) sugar
1 level tsp. yeast nutrient
port yeast
heavy sugar syrup, optional

Make as for Morello Cherry Wine (Dry), page 90. Use 3 lb. sugar initially and then dissolve the remaining ½ lb. in the must after pressing the pulp. The wine may be sweetened if necessary after fermentation has stopped.

BLACK DESSERT CHERRY WINE (Dry)

3 lb. (1·4 kg.) black dessert cherries
2 tsps. pectolase
1 gal. (4·5 l.) water
1 Campden tablet or 1 fl. oz. sulphite solution A
2 lb. (900 g.) sugar
1 level tsp. yeast nutrient
2 level tsps. citric acid
Pommard yeast

Make as for Morello Cherry Wine (Dry), page 91, adding the acid with the sugar, and yeast nutrient.

BLACK DESSERT CHERRY WINE (Sweet)

5 lb. (2·3 kg.) black dessert cherries
2 tsps. pectolase
1 gal. (4·5 l.) water
1 Campden tablet or 1 fl. oz. sulphite solution A
2½ lb. (1·3 kg.) sugar
1 level tsp. yeast nutrient
port yeast
2 level tsps. citric acid

Make as for Morello Cherry Wine (Dry), page 91, adding the acid before straining the wine. Use 2 lb. sugar initially, then dissolve ½ lb. sugar in the must after pressing the pulp.

CURRANTS

Three varieties of currant are grown in Britain, white, black and red. As each has a different chemical structure, the wines from each variety will have different characteristics. All currants should be left on the bushes for 3–4 weeks after changing colour. This will ensure a maximum sugar content with minimum acid. Unless the fruit is ripe right through, the wine will have a 'green' taste. Bought fruit should be chosen for its ripeness and quality.

Both white and red currants may be used for a dry table wine. Black currants have a very strong flavour and are therefore better suited to a sweet wine. A mixture of red and black currants may be used for a dry table wine, for example in the ratio one-third black to two-thirds red. The method of wine production is the same for all varieties.

WHITE CURRANT WINE (Dry)

2½ lb. (1·2 kg.) white currants
1 tsp. pectolase
1 gal. (4·5 l.) water
1 Campden tablet or 1 fl. oz. sulphite solution A
2¾ lb. (1·3 kg.) sugar
1 level tsp. yeast nutrient
Chablis yeast

Put the currants into a fermentation vessel and crush them. Add the pectolase and 6 pt. cold water. Add a crushed Campden tablet or 1 fl. oz. sulphite solution A, cover the vessel and leave for 24 hours.

Heat 2 pt. water and in it dissolve the sugar and yeast nutrient. Allow to cool to 80°F (27°C) and then add it to the currants. Add an active yeast culture, stir, cover the vessel closely and ferment on the pulp in a temperature of 70°F (21°C) for 3 days, stirring twice daily. Press the pulp, then strain into a clean 1-gal. jar, fit an airlock and ferment at 65°F (18°C) to dryness. Rack and store in a cool place.

WHITE CURRANT WINE (Sweet)

3 lb. (1·4 kg.) white currants
1 tsp. pectolase
1 gal. (4·5 l.) water
1 Campden tablet or 1 fl. oz. sulphite solution A
3½ lb. (1·6 kg.) sugar
1 level tsp. yeast nutrient
Tokay yeast
heavy sugar syrup, optional

Make as for White Currant Wine (Dry), above. Use 3 lb. sugar initially then dissolve the remaining ½ lb. in the must after pressing the pulp. Rack the wine again when fermentation stops and sweeten with heavy syrup if necessary.

RED CURRANT ROSE

2 lb. (900 g.) red currants
1 tsp. pectolase
1 gal. (4·5 l.) water
1 Campden tablet or 1 fl. oz. sulphite solution A
2¾ lb. (1·3 kg.) sugar
1 level tsp. yeast nutrient
Bordeaux yeast

Make as for White Currant Wine (Dry), page 93, but ferment the pulp for only 2 days.

RED CURRANT WINE (Sweet)

3 lb. (1·4 kg.) red currants
1 tsp. pectolase
1 gal. (4·5 l.) water
1 Campden tablet or 1 fl. oz. sulphite solution A
3½ lb. (1·6 kg.) sugar
1 level tsp. yeast nutrient
all purpose yeast

Make as for White Currant Wine (Sweet), page 93.

RED AND BLACK CURRANT WINE (Dry)

1½ lb. (675 g.) red currants
½ lb. (225 g.) black currants
1 tsp. pectolase
1 gal. (4·5 l.) water
1 Campden tablet or 1 fl. oz. sulphite solution A
2½ lb. (1·2 kg.) sugar
½ pt. (300 ml.) red grape concentrate
1 level tsp. yeast nutrient
Pommard yeast

Make as for White Currant Wine (Dry), page 93, dissolving the grape concentrate in the hot water with the sugar and yeast nutrient.

RED AND BLACK CURRANT WINE (Sweet)

2 lb. (900 g.) red currants
1 lb. (450 g.) black currants
1 tsp. pectolase
1 gal. (4·5 l.) water
1 Campden tablet or 1 fl. oz. sulphite solution A
2½ lb. (1·2 kg.) sugar
1 pt. (0·57 l.) red grape concentrate
1 level tsp. yeast nutrient
all purpose yeast

Make as for White Currant Wine (Sweet), page 93, using 2 lb. sugar initially and dissolving the remaining ½ lb. in the must after pressing; dissolve the grape concentrate in the hot water with the sugar and yeast nutrient.

BLACK CURRANT WINE (Sweet)

2½ lb. (1·2 kg.) black currants
1 tsp. pectolase
1 gal. (4·5 l.) water
1 Campden tablet or 1 fl. oz. sulphite solution A
2½ lb. (1·2 kg.) sugar
1 pt. (0·57 l.) red grape concentrate
1 level tsp. yeast nutrient
all purpose yeast

Make as for Red and Black Currant Wine (Sweet), above.

ELDERBERRIES

Elderberries make a very good table wine, but as the fruit contains a high proportion of tannin the wine is liable to be too astringent. To prevent this happening, keep the quantity of fruit in the must to a minimum and make up the body of the wine by adding another ingredient such as runner beans. Take care also to use only the correct varieties of elderberry; those which have red stalks and large clusters of berries are best.

ELDERBERRY AND RUNNER BEAN WINE (Dry)

1 lb. (450 g.) runner beans
1 gal. (4·5 l.) water
2 lb. (900 g.) elderberries
1 tsp. pectolase
1 level tsp. citric acid
1 Campden tablet or 1 fl. oz. sulphite solution A
2¾ lb. (1·3 kg.) sugar
1 level tsp. yeast nutrient
Pommard yeast

String the beans and, if they are old, break them into pieces by hand; slice young beans with a knife. Do not cut old beans as this would release too much starch into the water. Cook them in boiling water but do not add salt. Drain off the liquor and make it up to 6 pt. with water; the cooked beans may be eaten as a vegetable.

Crush the elderberries in a fermentation vessel. Pour the cold bean liquor over the elderberries and add the pectolase and citric acid. Sulphite the must with a crushed Campden tablet or 1 fl. oz. sulphite solution A; cover the vessel and leave for 24 hours.

Heat 2 pt. water and in it dissolve the sugar and yeast nutrient. Cool it to 80°F (27°C) and add it to the elderberries. Add the active yeast culture, stir, cover closely and ferment the pulp at 70°F (21°C) for 2 days. Strain the must into a clean 1-gal. jar, fit an airlock and ferment at 65°F (18°C) until the wine is dry. Rack and store in a cool place.

ELDERBERRY AND RUNNER BEAN WINE (Sweet) 1

1 lb. (450 g.) runner beans
1 gal. (4·5 l.) water
2½ lb. (1·2 kg.) elderberries
1 tsp. pectolase
¼ oz. (7 g.) citric acid
1 lb. (450 g.) sultanas
1 Campden tablet or 1 fl. oz. sulphite solution A
3 lb. (1·4 kg.) sugar
1 level tsp. yeast nutrient
all purpose yeast
heavy sugar syrup, optional

String the beans and if old break them into pieces by hand; slice young beans with a knife. Do not cut old beans as this would release too much starch into the water.

9 Pectin test, showing the
cloudy wine prior to testing,
the wine after adding
methylated spirit and, finally,
the clear red wine after
treatment with a pectin
destroying enzyme.

10 For the first, vigorous
fermentation the must often
has to be divided between
two jars.

11 A selection of earthenware jars for fermentation.

12 When racking, tilt the jar slightly to allow the last drops to syphon off.

Cook them in boiling water but do not add salt. Drain off the liquor and make it up to 6 pt. with water; the cooked beans may be eaten as a vegetable.

Crush the elderberries in a fermentation vessel. Pour the cold bean liquor over the elderberries and add the pectolase and citric acid; chop the sultanas and add to the must. Sulphite the must with a crushed Campden tablet or 1 fl. oz. sulphite solution; cover and leave the vessel for 24 hours.

Heat 2 pt. water and in it dissolve 2½ lb. sugar and the yeast nutrient. Cool it to 80°F (27°C) and add it to the elderberries. Add the active yeast culture, stir, cover closely and ferment the pulp at 70°F (21°C) for 3 days. Strain the must, add the remaining ½ lb. sugar and fill the wine into a clean 1-gal. jar. Fit an airlock and ferment at 65°F (18°C); the wine may be fed with heavy sugar syrup when the gravity drops to 5 (1·005). Rack and store in a cool place.

ELDERBERRY AND RUNNER BEAN WINE (Sweet) 2

1 lb. (450 g.) runner beans
1 gal. (4·5 l.) water
3 lb. (1·4 kg.) elderberries
1 tsp. pectolase
2 level tsps. citric acid
½ lb. (225 g.) sultanas
1 Campden tablet or 1 fl. oz. sulphite solution A
2½ lb. (1·2 kg.) sugar
1 pt. (0·57 l.) red grape concentrate
1 level tsp. yeast nutrient
all purpose yeast
heavy sugar syrup, optional

Make as for the previous recipe but ferment the pulp for 2 days only.

GOOSEBERRIES

Unripe gooseberries make an excellent dry, white table wine. The berries must not be picked until they are fully developed or they will give the wine a musty flavour, but if picked while still green they will give it a crisp but balanced acidity. Red gooseberries may also be used, picked when they show the first signs of colour.

For a sweet gooseberry wine the berries must be sound and whole but well ripened. The colour pictures facing page 17 show the different stages of ripeness.

It is not necessary to top and tail the gooseberries for wine.

GOOSEBERRY WINE (Dry)

2½ lb. (1·2 kg.) green gooseberries
1 tsp. pectolase
1 gal. (4·5 l.) water
1 Campden tablet or 1 fl. oz. sulphite solution A
2½ lb. (1·2 kg.) sugar
1 level tsp. yeast nutrient
½ level tsp. grape tannin
Chablis yeast

Put the gooseberries through a mincer, using a plate with ¼-in. holes. Put the pulp into a fermentation vessel, add the pectolase and 6 pt. cold water. Sulphite with a crushed Campden tablet or 1 fl. oz. sulphite solution A, cover the vessel and leave for 24 hours.

Heat 2 pt. water and in it dissolve the sugar, yeast nutrient and tannin; allow it to cool to 80°F (27°C) then add to the gooseberries. Add an active yeast culture, stir, cover closely and ferment the pulp for 2 days at 70°F (21°C). Press the pulp and strain the juice into a clean 1-gal. jar; fit an airlock and ferment to dryness. Rack and store in a cool place.

GOOSEBERRY WINE (Sweet)

4 lb. (1·8 kg.) ripe gooseberries
1 tsp. pectolase
1 gal. (4·5 l.) water
1 Campden tablet or 1 fl. oz. sulphite solution A
3 lb. (1·4 kg.) sugar
1 level tsp. yeast nutrient
Sauternes yeast
citric acid, optional

Make as for Gooseberry Wine (Dry); add 2½ lb. sugar initially and the remaining ½ lb. after straining the pulp. Check the acidity and add a little citric acid if necessary.

GRAPES

Grapes are the ideal fruit for winemaking. See Chapter 10.

WHITE GRAPE WINE (Dry) 1

20–22 lb. (9–9·9 kg.) white grapes
1 Campden tablet or 1 fl. oz. sulphite solution A
½ lb. (225 g.) sugar, approx.
tartaric acid, optional
Chablis yeast

Crush the grapes and press out the juice, which should make about 1 gal. Retain the pulp for a second run. Add a crushed Campden tablet or the sulphite solution to the juice and leave for 24 hours. Rack the must into a clean jar, leaving behind the lees, and add sugar until the gravity is 80 (1·080). Retain the lees for the second run. Adjust the acidity if necessary to about 3·5 p.p.t.; the must should have a sharp acid taste but if the acid content is too high, adjust as described on page 47.

Add the active yeast culture and divide the wine between two jars; fit airlocks and ferment at 70°F (21°C) until the vigorous fermentation subsides. Now fill one jar gently from the other, fit an airlock again and continue to ferment, at 65°F (18°C), to dryness. Rack and store in a cool place.

WHITE GRAPE WINE (Dry) 2
(second run from the pulp)

pulp from the first pressing
water
lees from the juice of the first pressing
2 tsps. pectolase
2 Campden tablets or 1½ fl. oz. sulphite solution A
2 lb. (900 g.) sugar, approx.
tartaric acid, optional
Chablis yeast

Put the pressed pulp in a fermentation vessel and add 6 pt. cold water. Add the pectolase and sulphite and stir well; cover and leave for 24 hours. Make up the lees from the first pressing to 2 pt. with cold water and add to the pulp.

Stir the must again and strain off 1½ pt. juice. Use the hydrometer to take a gravity reading and calculate the amount of sugar needed to bring the gravity to 85 (1·085). Heat the strained juice and dissolve in it the calculated amount of sugar; cool to 80°F (27°C) and add to the pulp. Check the acidity and make any necessary adjustment with the tartaric acid. Add the active yeast culture and cover the vessel closely. Ferment the pulp for 3–4 days, stirring twice daily. Then press the pulp through a cloth and pour the juice into a clean 1-gal. jar, fit an airlock and ferment at 65°F (18°C) to dryness. Rack and store in a cool place.

RED GRAPE WINE (Dry) 1

20–22 lb. (9–9·9 kg.) black grapes
1 tsp. pectolase
2 Campden tablets or 1½ fl. oz. sulphite solution A
½ lb. (225 g.) sugar, approx.
tartaric acid, optional
Pommard yeast

Crush the grapes in a fermentation vessel, add the pectolase and crushed Campden tablets or sulphite solution, cover and leave for 24 hours. Strain 1 pt. juice from the pulp and take a gravity reading. Estimate the amount of sugar required to raise the gravity to 90 (1·090) and make a note for future reference. Check the acidity and adjust it if necessary with tartaric acid. Return the juice to the pulp and add an active yeast culture. Stir well, cover the vessel and ferment the pulp for 4 days at 70°F (21°C), stirring twice daily.

   Strain or press the pulp, dissolve the necessary amount of sugar in the juice and pour into a clean 1-gal. jar. If there is insufficient liquid to fill the jar, top up with cold water. Fit an airlock and ferment at 65°F (18°C) to dryness. Rack and store in a cool place.

ROSE GRAPE WINE

20–22 lb. (9–9·9 kg.) black grapes
1 tsp. pectolase
2 Campden tablets or 1½ fl. oz. sulphite solution A
½ lb. (225 g.) sugar, approx.
tartaric acid, optional
all purpose yeast

Crush the grapes in a fermentation vessel, add the pectolase and crushed Campden tablets or sulphite solution, cover and leave for 24 hours. Strain 1 pt. juice from the pulp and take a gravity reading; estimate the amount of sugar required to raise the gravity to 85 (1·085) and make a note for future reference. Check the acidity and adjust it if necessary with tartaric acid. Return the juice to the pulp and add an active yeast culture. Stir well, cover the vessel and ferment the pulp at

70°F (21°C), stirring twice daily until sufficient colour has been extracted (at least 2 days). Press the pulp, dissolve the necessary amount of sugar in the juice and pour it into a clean 1-gal. jar. Top up with cold water if necessary, fit an airlock and ferment at 65°F (18°C) to dryness. Rack and store in a cool place.

GRAPE WINE (Sweet)

Follow the recipes for White Grape Wine (Dry) 1 and 2 but add enough sugar to raise the gravity to 100 (1·100), feeding the wine with heavy sugar syrup when the gravity drops to 5 (1·005). After the first racking, sulphite sweet wines with an extra ½ Campden tablet or ½ fl. oz. sulphite solution A.

WHITE GRAPE WINE (Dry) 3
(using water with the grapes)

10 lb. (4·5 kg.) white grapes
4 pt. (2·25 l.) water, approx.
1 Campden tablet or 1 fl. oz. sulphite solution A
1½ lb. (680 g.) sugar, approx.
tartaric acid, optional
Hock yeast

Crush the grapes, press out the juice and make it up to 1 gal. with cold water. Add a crushed Campden tablet or the sulphite solution, cover the vessel and leave for 24 hours. Rack the must into a clean jar, leaving behind the lees, and add sugar until the gravity is 85 (1·085). Adjust the acidity if necessary to about 3·5 p.p.t. Add the active yeast culture and divide the wine between two jars; fit airlocks and ferment at 70°F (21°C) until the vigorous fermentation subsides. Now fill one jar gently from the other, fit an airlock again and continue to ferment, at 65°F (18°C), to dryness. Rack and store in a cool place.

RED GRAPE WINE (Dry) 2
(using water with the grapes)

10 lb. (4·5 kg.) black grapes
1 pt. (0·57 l.) red grape concentrate
4 pt. (2·25 l.) water
1 tsp. pectolase
1 Campden tablet or 1 fl. oz. sulphite solution A
tartaric acid, optional
Bordeaux yeast
1½ lb. (680 g.) sugar, approx.

Crush the grapes in the fermentation vessel. Dissolve the grape concentrate in the water, pour over the grapes and add the pectolase. Add a crushed Campden tablet or the sulphite solution, cover and leave for 24 hours. Strain 1 pt. juice from the pulp and take a gravity reading. Estimate the amount of sugar required to raise the gravity to 90 (1·090) and make a note for future reference. Check the acidity and adjust it if necessary with tartaric acid. Return the juice to the pulp and add an active yeast culture. Stir well, cover the vessel and ferment the pulp for 4 days at 70°F (21°C), stirring twice daily.

Strain or press the pulp, dissolve the necessary amount of sugar in the juice and pour into a clean 1-gal. jar. If there is insufficient liquid to fill the jar, top up with cold water. Fit an airlock and ferment at 65°F (18°C) to dryness. Rack and store in a cool place.

GRAPE CONCENTRATE

Concentrated grape juice is freely available to amateur winemakers, though the quality of the product varies. Good quality concentrate makes a useful wine; red concentrate tends to produce a better wine than white. Full directions for use are supplied by the various producers.

Wine made from grape concentrate is seldom of the same quality as wine made from fresh grape juice but it has one big advantage – it can be drunk when still young and is quite palatable. It is useful for the beginner to make as it provides a wine that can be drunk while wines made from fresh fruit are still maturing.

GRAPEFRUIT

Avoid including the white pith or the pips of citrus fruit in wine, as these will make it very bitter.

GRAPEFRUIT WINE (Dry)

6 grapefruit
1 tsp. pectolase
1 gal. (4·5 l.) water, approx.
1 Campden tablet or 1 fl. oz. sulphite solution A
2¾ lb. (1·3 kg.) sugar
1 level tsp. yeast nutrient
all purpose yeast

Cut the fruit in half and extract the juice with the help of a lemon squeezer. Leave in the juice any pulp from the fruit, but take out all pips. Measure the juice and put it in a fermentation vessel with the pectolase and cold water to make the volume up to 6 pt. Add a crushed Campden tablet or 1 fl. oz. sulphite solution. Pare the rind from two of the grapefruit skins, taking care not to include any white pith. Add this rind to the juice, cover the vessel and leave for 24 hours.

Heat 2 pt. water and in it dissolve the sugar and yeast nutrient. Allow it to cool to 80°F (27°C) and pour it into the juice. Add the active yeast culture, stir and ferment at 70°F (21°C) for 3 days. Strain the wine into a clean 1-gal. jar, fit an airlock and ferment at 65°F (18°C) to dryness. Rack and store in a cool place.

GRAPEFRUIT WINE (Sweet)

8 grapefruit
1 tsp. pectolase
1 gal. (4·5 l.) water, approx.
½ lb. (225 g.) sultanas
1 Campden tablet or 1 fl. oz. sulphite solution A
3½ lb. (1·6 kg.) sugar
1 level tsp. yeast nutrient
½ level tsp. grape tannin
Tokay yeast

Cut the fruit and extract the juice as for Grapefruit Wine (Dry), above. Measure the juice and put it in the fermentation vessel with the pectolase and cold water to make the volume up to 6 pt. Chop the sultanas, add them to the juice and sulphite with a crushed Campden tablet or the sulphite solution. Add the pared rind of two of the grapefruit, cover and leave for 24 hours. Heat 2 pt. water and in it dissolve 3 lb. sugar, the yeast nutrient and the tannin. Allow it to cool to 80°F (27°C) and pour it into the juice. Add the active yeast culture, stir and ferment for 3 days at 70°F (21°C). Strain the wine, add the remaining ½ lb. sugar, pour it into a clean 1-gal. jar, fit an airlock and ferment at 65°F (18°C). When fermentation stops, rack the wine and store in a cool place.

GREENGAGES

Greengages contain a certain amount of malic acid and a malo-lactic fermentation may therefore be encouraged; this will reduce much of the harder malic acid to softer lactic acid.

GREENGAGE WINE (Dry)

2 lb. (900 g.) greengages
2 tsps. pectolase
1 gal. (4·5 l.) water
1 Campden tablet or 1 fl. oz. sulphite solution A
2¾ lb. (1·3 kg.) sugar
1 level tsp. yeast nutrient
all purpose yeast

Put the fruit in a fermentation vessel and bruise it, taking care not to break the stones. Add the pectolase and 6 pt. cold water, then stir in a crushed Campden tablet or sulphite solution. Cover the vessel and leave for 24 hours.

Heat 2 pt. water and in it dissolve the sugar and yeast nutrient; allow it to cool to 80°F (27°C), then add it to the greengages. Add the active yeast culture, stir and cover closely. Ferment the pulp for 24 hours, stirring 2–3 times during the day.

With well scrubbed hands, remove as many stones as possible, then ferment the pulp for 2 days more, stirring twice daily. Strain the wine into a clean 1-gal. jar, fit an airlock and ferment at 65°F (18°C) to dryness. Rack and store in a cool place.

GREENGAGE WINE (Sweet)

3 lb. (1·4 kg.) greengages
2 tsps. pectolase
1 gal. (4·5 l.) water
½ lb. (225 g.) sultanas
1 Campden tablet or 1 fl. oz. sulphite solution A
3½ lb. (1·6 kg.) sugar
1 level tsp. yeast nutrient
Sauternes yeast

Put the fruit in a fermentation vessel and bruise it as for Greengage Wine (Dry), above. Add the pectolase, 6 pt. cold water and the chopped sultanas. Add the Campden tablet or sulphite solution, cover and leave for 24 hours.

Heat 2 pt. water and in it dissolve 3 lb. sugar and the yeast nutrient. Continue as for Greengage Wine (Dry) and add the remaining sugar after straining the wine.

LEMONS

As with all citrus fruit, the pith and pips of lemons will make a wine bitter; these should therefore be kept out of the must.

LEMON WINE (Dry)

8 lemons
1 gal. (4·5 l.) water, approx.
½ lb. (225 g.) sultanas
1 tsp. pectolase
1 Campden tablet or 1 fl. oz. sulphite solution A
2½ lb. (1·2 kg.) sugar
1 level tsp. yeast nutrient
all purpose yeast

Cut the lemons in half and extract the juice with a lemon squeezer. Leave any pulp particles in the juice but discard all pips. Measure the juice and make it up to 6 pt. with cold water. Chop the sultanas, put them in the fermentation vessel and add the juice and water and pectolase. Add a crushed Campden tablet or sulphite solution, cover the vessel and leave for 24 hours.

Heat 2 pt. water and in it dissolve the sugar and yeast nutrient; allow to cool to 80°F (27°C) and stir it into the must. Add an active yeast culture, cover closely and ferment at 70°F (21°C) for 4 days. Strain or press the wine, pour it into a clean 1-gal. jar, fit an airlock and ferment it at 65°F (18°C) to dryness. Rack and store in a cool place.

LEMON WINE (Sweet)

10 lemons
1 gal. (4·5 l.) water, approx.
1 lb. (450 g.) sultanas
1 tsp. pectolase
1 Campden tablet or 1 fl. oz. sulphite solution A
3½ lb. (1·6 kg.) sugar
1 level tsp. yeast nutrient
Tokay yeast

Make as for Lemon Wine (Dry), above, using only 3 lb. sugar initially and adding the remainder after straining the wine.

LOGANBERRIES

LOGANBERRY WINE (Dry)

2½ lb. (1·2 kg.) ripe loganberries
1 tsp. pectolase
1 gal. (4·5 l.) water
1 Campden tablet or 1 fl. oz. sulphite solution A
2¾ lb. (1·3 kg.) sugar
1 level tsp. yeast nutrient
Pommard yeast

Put the loganberries in a fermentation vessel and crush them. Add the pectolase and 6 pt. cold water. Stir in a crushed Campden tablet or the sulphite solution, cover the vessel and leave for 24 hours.

Heat 2 pt. water and in it dissolve the sugar and yeast nutrient. Cool it to 80°F (27°C) and add it to the loganberries. Add an active yeast culture, stir, cover the vessel closely and ferment the pulp at 70°F (21°C) for 2 days, stirring twice daily. Strain the wine into a clean 1-gal. jar, fit an airlock and ferment at 65°F (18°C) to dryness. Rack and store in a cool place.

LOGANBERRY WINE (Sweet)

3 lb. (1·4 kg.) loganberries
1 tsp. pectolase
1 gal. (4·5 l.) water
1 Campden tablet or 1 fl. oz. sulphite solution A
3¼ lb. (1·5 kg.) sugar
½ pt. (280 ml.) red grape concentrate
1 level tsp. yeast nutrient
all purpose yeast

Put the loganberries in the fermentation vessel and crush them. Add the pectolase and 6 pt. cold water. Stir in the crushed Campden tablet or the sulphite solution, cover the vessel and leave for 24 hours.

Heat 2 pt. water and in it dissolve 2¾ lb. sugar, the grape concentrate and yeast nutrient. Cool to 80°F (27°C) and add it to the loganberries. Add an active yeast culture, stir, cover the vessel and ferment at 70°F (21°C) for 2 days, stirring twice daily. Strain the wine, dissolve in it the remaining ½ lb. sugar and pour it into a clean 1-gal. jar. Fit an airlock and ferment at 65°F (18°C). When fermentation ceases rack and store in a cool place.

MULBERRIES

Mulberries have a very strong flavour and are therefore not suitable for a dry wine. The berries must be absolutely black when gathered or the wine will be too acid and 'green' tasting. Once it is ripe, gather the fruit quickly or the birds will take it.

MULBERRY WINE (Sweet)

3 lb. (1·4 kg.) mulberries
1 tsp. pectolase
1 gal. (4·5 l.) water
1 Campden tablet or 1 fl. oz. sulphite solution A
3½ lb. (1·6 kg.) sugar
1 level tsp. yeast nutrient
all purpose yeast
heavy sugar syrup, optional

Make as for Blackberry Wine (Sweet), page 90.

ORANGES

An advantage of making wine from oranges is that it can be made all through the year. Nevertheless, the quality and juice content of the fruit vary considerably, so bear this in mind when buying fruit. Your greengrocer will be only too pleased to advise you.

Oranges make a very good table wine if only a minimum amount of peel is included in the must, and if the acid content is adjusted carefully. Some recipes include peel which has been dried in the oven but this strong flavour tends to overpower the delicate flavour of the fruit juice and dried peel should not be used if you are making a table wine.

ORANGE WINE (Dry)

15 sweet oranges
1 gal. (4·5 l.) water, approx.
1 tsp. pectolase
1 Campden tablet or 1 fl. oz. sulphite solution A
2½ lb. (1·2 kg.) sugar
¼ oz. (7 g.) citric acid
1 level tsp. yeast nutrient
Chablis yeast

Halve the fruit and extract the juice with a lemon squeezer. Leave any fruit pulp in the juice but take out all pips. Measure the juice and make it up to 6 pt. with cold water. Pare the rind thinly from 3 orange skins, making sure there is no white pith attached. Put the juice, water, rind and pectolase in the fermentation vessel and stir in a crushed Campden tablet or the sulphite solution. Cover the vessel and leave for 24 hours.

Heat 2 pt. water and dissolve in it the sugar, acid and yeast nutrient. Cool it to 80°F (27°C) and pour it into the fermentation vessel. Add the active yeast culture, stir, cover the vessel closely and ferment at 70°F (21°C) for 4 days. Strain the wine into a clean 1-gal. jar, fit an airlock and ferment it at 65°F (18°C) to dryness. Rack and store in a cool place.

ORANGE WINE (Sweet) 1

20 sweet oranges
1 gal. (4·5 l.) water, approx.
1 tsp. pectolase
1 Campden tablet or 1 fl. oz. sulphite solution A
3½ lb. (1·6 kg.) sugar
¼ oz. (7 g.) citric acid
½ level tsp. grape tannin
1 level tsp. yeast nutrient
Sauternes yeast

Halve the fruit and extract the juice as for Orange Wine (Dry), above. Make it up to 6 pt. with cold water and put it in the fermentation vessel with the pared rind of 5 oranges. Stir in the pectolase, a crushed Campden tablet or the sulphite solution, cover and leave for 24 hours.

Heat 2 pt. water and in it dissolve 3 lb. sugar, the acid, tannin and yeast nutrient. Cool it to 80°F (27°C) and pour it into the must. Add the active yeast culture, stir, cover the vessel closely and ferment at 70°F (21°C) for 4 days. Strain the must, dissolve in it the remaining sugar and pour it into a clean 1-gal. jar; fit an airlock and ferment at 65°F (18°C). When fermentation is complete rack and store in a cool place.

ORANGE WINE (Sweet) 2

20 sweet oranges
1 gal. (4·5 l.) water, approx.
1 lb. (450 g.) sultanas
1 tsp. pectolase
1 Campden tablet or 1 fl. oz. sulphite solution A
3 lb. (1·4 kg.) sugar
¼ oz. (7 g.) citric acid
½ level tsp. grape tannin
1 level tsp. yeast nutrient
sherry yeast

Halve the fruit and extract the juice as for Orange Wine (Dry), page 108. Make it up to 6 pt. with cold water and put it in the fermentation vessel with the chopped sultanas, the pared rind of 5 oranges, the pectolase and a crushed Campden tablet or the sulphite solution. Cover and leave for 24 hours. Heat 2 pt. water and in it dissolve 2½ lb. sugar, the acid, tannin and yeast nutrient. Cool it to 80°F (27°C) and pour it into the must. Add the active yeast culture and ferment at 70°F (21°C) for 5 days. Strain the must, add the remaining sugar and pour it into a clean 1-gal. jar. Fit an airlock and ferment at 65°F (18°C). When fermentation is complete rack and store in a cool place.

TANGERINE WINE (Dry)

25 tangerines
1 tsp. pectolase
¼ oz. (7 g.) citric acid
7 pt. (4 l.) water
1 Campden tablet or 1 fl. oz. sulphite solution A
2½ lb. (1·2 kg.) sugar
½ level tsp. grape tannin
1 level tsp. yeast nutrient
all purpose yeast

Peel the tangerines and remove all the white pith from the fruit segments. Cut the fruit and remove all pips. Put the fruit in a fermentation vessel and crush it. Add the pectolase, citric acid and 5 pt. cold water and sulphite with a crushed Campden tablet or the sulphite solution. Cover and leave for 24 hours. Heat 2 pt. water and dissolve in it the sugar, tannin and yeast nutrient. Cool it to 80°F (27°C) and add to the fruit. Stir, add the active yeast culture, cover and ferment the pulp for 3 days at 70°F (21°C). Strain or press the wine and pour it into a clean 1-gal. jar; fit an airlock and ferment at 65°F (18°C) to dryness. Rack and store in a cool place.

PEACHES

Peach wine is considered to be second in quality only to a grape wine. Fresh peaches in particular make a very attractive wine. The fruit should be well ripened; if unripe fruit is used the wine will have an unpleasant 'green' taste.

PEACH WINE (Dry)

1½ lb. (675 g.) fresh peaches or ½ lb. (225 g.) dried peaches
1 gal. (4·5 l.) water
2 tsps. pectolase
1 level tsp. citric acid
1 Campden tablet or 1 fl. oz. sulphite solution A
2½ lb. (1·2 kg.) sugar
1 level tsp. yeast nutrient
1 level tsp. grape tannin
Chablis yeast

If using dried peaches, cut them up, cover with water and soak overnight; then boil them in the soaking water until soft. Drain them, measure the cooking liquor and make it up to 6 pt. with cold water. If using fresh peaches, peel them and remove the stones, chop the fruit and put it in the fermentation vessel. Add 6 pt. cold water (if using dried fruit add the 6 pt. water and cooking liquor combined). Add the pectolase, acid and a crushed Campden tablet or the sulphite solution. Cover the vessel and leave for 24 hours.

Heat 2 pt. water and in it dissolve the sugar, yeast nutrient and tannin. Cool it to 80°F (27°C) and pour it over the peaches. Add an active yeast culture, stir and cover the vessel closely. Ferment the pulp at 70°F (21°C) for 3 days, stirring twice daily. Strain or press the wine and pour it into a clean 1-gal. jar. Fit an airlock and ferment it at 65°F (18°C) to dryness. Rack and store in a cool place.

PEACH WINE (Sweet)

2 lb. (900 g.) fresh peaches or ¾ lb. (340 g.) dried peaches
1 gal. (4·5 l.) water
2 tsps. pectolase
1 level tsp. citric acid
1 Campden tablet or 1 fl. oz. sulphite solution A
3½ lb. (1·6 kg.) sugar
1 level tsp. yeast nutrient
1 level tsp. grape tannin
Tokay yeast
heavy sugar syrup, optional

Make as for Peach Wine (Dry), page 110, using 3 lb. sugar initially and dissolving the rest in the must after straining the pulp. This wine may be fed with heavy sugar syrup when the gravity has dropped to 5 (1·005).

PEARS

Wine made from ripe pears is disappointing; it is drinkable but it lacks quality. Using fully grown but unripe pears, however, the result is a very good wine.

PEAR WINE (Dry)

pears (as available)
For each 1 gal. pear juice:
1 Campden tablet or 1 fl. oz. sulphite solution A
1 level tsp. citric acid
1 tsp. pectolase
2 lb. (900 g.) sugar, approx.
1 level tsp. yeast nutrient
all purpose yeast

Mince the pears, press the pulp and run each gallon of juice straight into a 1-gal. jar containing a crushed Campden tablet or 1 fl. oz. sulphite solution, to prevent discoloration. Add the citric acid and pectolase, cover and leave for 24 hours. During this time pulp will settle on the bottom of the jar; after 24 hours rack the juice into a clean jar, leaving the sediment behind. Take a gravity reading of the juice and estimate the amount of sugar required to raise the gravity to 85. Dissolve this sugar in the juice, add the yeast nutrient and the active yeast culture. Stir well and divide the must between two 1-gal. jars; fit airlocks and ferment at 70°F (21°C). When the first vigorous fermentation stops, fill one jar gently from the other, pouring slowly to avoid frothing. Re-fit the airlock and ferment at 65°F (18°C) to dryness. Rack and store in a cool place.

PEAR WINE (Sweet)

pears (as available)
For each 1 gal. pear juice:
1 Campden tablet or 1 fl. oz. sulphite solution A
1 level tsp. citric acid
1 tsp. pectolase
1 lb. (450 g.) sultanas
3 lb. (1·4 kg.) sugar, approx.
1 level tsp. yeast nutrient
all purpose yeast
heavy sugar syrup, optional

Mince the pears, press the pulp and add to each gallon of juice a crushed Campden tablet or 1 fl. oz. sulphite solution, the acid and pectolase. Chop the sultanas, put them in a fermentation vessel, pour over 1 gal. sulphited pear juice, cover and leave for 24 hours. Dissolve 2½ lb. sugar in the juice, add the yeast nutrient and an active yeast culture. Stir well, cover the vessel closely and ferment at 70°F (21°C) for 4 days. Strain the must, add the remaining ½ lb. sugar and pour it into a clean 1-gal. jar; fit an airlock and ferment at 65°F (18°C). When fermentation stops, rack the wine, feed with heavy sugar syrup if necessary and store in a cool place.

PINEAPPLES

Pineapple has a distinctive flavour that makes it better suited to a sweet wine than a dry.

PINEAPPLE WINE (Sweet)

3 lb. (1·4 kg.) pineapples
1 level tsp. citric acid
2 tsps. pectolase
1 gal. (4·5 l.) water
1 Campden tablet or 1 fl. oz. sulphite solution A
3½ lb. (1·6 kg.) sugar
1 level tsp. yeast nutrient
all purpose yeast
heavy sugar syrup

Use pineapples that are as ripe as possible. Discard the top and bottom of the fruit, remove the peel and chop the flesh into small pieces. Put the fruit in a fermentation vessel, add the citric acid and pectolase and pour over 6 pt. cold water. Stir in a crushed Campden tablet or the sulphite solution, cover and leave for 24 hours.

Heat 2 pt. water and in it dissolve 3 lb. sugar and the yeast nutrient. Cool to 80°F (27°C) and pour into the pineapple must. Add an active yeast culture and ferment the pulp at 70°F (21°C) for 3 days. Press the pulp and dissolve the remaining ½ lb. sugar in the juice. Pour it into a clean 1-gal. jar, fit an airlock and ferment at 65°F (18°C). When fermentation stops, rack into a clean jar, sweeten to taste with heavy sugar syrup and store in a cool place.

PLUMS

Victoria plums make a delicately flavoured, lightly coloured wine. Purple plums like Monarch or Early Rivers give a wine with a fuller flavour and a deeper colour. Yellow plums give a wine with a light golden colour. All require the same method of preparation but when making a sweet wine with Victoria plums, a higher proportion of fruit may be used. Plums contain a lot of pectin, so a pectin reducing enzyme should be used.

PLUM WINE (Dry)

2 lb. (900 g.) plums
2 tsps. pectolase
1 gal. (4·5 l.) water
1 Campden tablet or 1 fl. oz. sulphite solution A
2¾ lb. (1·3 kg.) sugar
1 level tsp. yeast nutrient
all purpose yeast

Select the fruit carefully, cut the plums in half and remove the stones. Put the fruit in a fermentation vessel and crush it. Add the pectolase and 6 pt. cold water and stir in a crushed Campden tablet or 1 fl. oz. sulphite solution. Cover and leave for 24 hours.

Heat 2 pt. water and in it dissolve the sugar and yeast nutrient. Cool to 80°F (27°C) and pour it over the fruit. Stir and add an active yeast culture. Cover the vessel and ferment the pulp for 3 days at 70°F (21°C), stirring twice daily. Strain the pulp through a coarse cloth and pour into a clean 1-gal. jar, fit an airlock and ferment at 65°F (18°C) to dryness. Rack and store in a cool place.

PLUM WINE (Sweet)

3 lb. (1·4 kg.) plums, or 4 lb. (1·8 kg.) Victorias
2 tsps. pectolase
7 pt. (4 l.) water
1 Campden tablet or 1 fl. oz. sulphite solution A
3½ lb. (1·6 kg.) sugar
1 level tsp. yeast nutrient
all purpose yeast
heavy sugar syrup, optional

Make as for Plum Wine (Dry), page 113, using 3 lb. sugar initially and adding the remainder to the must after straining. When fermentation stops, rack the wine into a clean jar and sweeten with heavy sugar syrup if necessary.

DAMSONS

Damsons have a strong plummy flavour and are therefore better suited to sweet wine than to dry. They contain a high proportion of pectin and addition of a pectin reducing enzyme is essential. As damsons also contain malic acid, a malo-lactic fermentation should be encouraged; this will reduce much of the harder malic acid to softer lactic acid. The wine should not be sulphited after fermentation.

DAMSON WINE (Dry)

2 lb. (900 g.) damsons
2 tsps. pectolase
1 gal. (4·5 l.) water
1 Campden tablet or 1 fl. oz. sulphite solution A
2¾ lb. (1·3 kg.) sugar
1 level tsp. yeast nutrient
Pommard or Burgundy yeast

Put the fruit into a fermentation vessel and bruise it, taking care not to break the stones. Add the pectolase and 6 pt. cold water, then stir in a crushed Campden tablet or the sulphite solution. Cover the vessel and leave it for 24 hours.

Heat 2 pt. water and in it dissolve the sugar and yeast nutrient, cool to 80°F (27°C), then add to the damsons. Add the active yeast culture, stir and cover the vessel closely. Ferment for 24 hours, stirring two or three times during the day. With well scrubbed hands, remove as many stones as possible. Ferment the pulp for 2 days more, stirring twice daily. Strain wine and pour into a clean 1-gal. jar, fit an airlock and ferment at 65°F (18°C) to dryness. Rack and store in a cool place.

DAMSON WINE (Sweet)

3 lb. (1·4 kg.) damsons
2 tsps. pectolase
1 gal. (4·5 l.) water
1 Campden tablet or 1 fl. oz. sulphite solution A
3½ lb. (1·6 kg.) sugar
1 level tsp. yeast nutrient
all purpose yeast
heavy sugar syrup, optional

Make as for Damson Wine (Dry), page 114, using 3 lb. sugar initially then adding
½ lb. after straining the must. When fermentation stops, rack the wine into a clean
jar and sweeten with heavy sugar syrup if necessary.

RASPBERRIES

Raspberries make a delightful medium sweet or sweet wine and a dry
wine can be made; their strong characteristic smell and flavour preclude
them from making a really good table wine. Raspberries have a rather
high acid content and in order to produce a balanced wine the quantity
of fruit used must be restricted. The fruit should be ripe and picked, if
possible, during a hot, dry spell.
  Raspberry wine will retain its fresh, fruity flavour for many years.

RASPBERRY WINE (Dry)

2 lb. (900 g.) raspberries
1 tsp. pectolase
1 gal. (4·5 l.) water
1 Campden tablet or 1 fl. oz. sulphite solution A
2¾ lb. (1·3 kg.) sugar
1 level tsp. yeast nutrient
all purpose yeast

Make as for Blackberry Wine (Dry), page 89. It will not be necessary to add acid
to a Raspberry Wine.

RASPBERRY WINE (Rosé)

2 lb. (900 g.) raspberries
1 tsp. pectolase
1 gal. (4·5 l.) water
1½ Campden tablets or 1½ fl. oz. sulphite solution A
3 lb. (1·4 kg.) sugar
1 level tsp. yeast nutrient
all purpose yeast
heavy sugar syrup

Make as for Blackberry Wine (Dry), page 89. When fermentation stops, rack the wine at intervals to stabilise it and add sugar syrup to raise the gravity to 4 or 5 (1·004–1·005). Finally sulphite with an extra ½ crushed Campden tablet or ½ fl. oz. sulphite solution per gal. and store in a cool place to mature.

RASPBERRY WINE (Sweet)

3 lb. (1·4 kg.) raspberries
1 tsp. pectolase
1 gal. (4·5 l.) water
1 Campden tablet or 1 fl. oz. sulphite solution A
3½ lb. (1·6 kg.) sugar
1 level tsp. yeast nutrient
Sauternes yeast
heavy sugar syrup, optional

Make as for Blackberry Wine (Sweet), page 90.

RHUBARB

Rhubarb is suitable for a dry, sweet or sparkling wine. Choose one of the less acid varieties and use young, fresh stalks.

RHUBARB WINE (Dry)

3 lb. (1·4 kg.) young rhubarb
1 gal. (4·5 l.) water
2 Campden tablets or 1½ fl. oz. sulphite solution A
2½ lb. (1·2 kg.) sugar
1 level tsp. yeast nutrient
all purpose yeast

Wash the stalks and remove the tops and bottoms. Cut the stalks into 2-in. lengths and bruise them with a mallet. Put the rhubarb in a fermentation vessel and pour on 6 pt. cold water. Add the crushed Campden tablets or the sulphite solution, cover closely and leave for 4 days, stirring daily.

Strain and discard the pulp. Heat 2 pt. water and in it dissolve the sugar and yeast nutrient. Cool it to 80°F (27°C) and add to the strained juice. Add an active yeast culture, stir well and divide the must between two 1-gal. jars. Fit airlocks and ferment at 70°F (21°C) until the first vigorous fermentation subsides. Gently fill one jar from the other, re-fit an airlock and ferment at 65°F (18°C) to dryness. Rack and store in a cool place.

RHUBARB WINE (Sweet)

4 lb. (1·8 kg.) rhubarb
1 gal. (4·5 l.) water
2 Campden tablets or 1½ fl. oz. sulphite solution A
3½ lb. (1·6 kg.) sugar
1 level tsp. yeast nutrient
all purpose yeast

Make as for Rhubarb Wine (Dry), above, using 3 lb. sugar initially and adding the remainder to one jar of the fermenting wine before combining both jars for the final fermentation.

SLOES

Sloes are the fruit of the blackthorn. As they are very acid and astringent they should be as ripe as possible when gathered. A number of hybrid berries in the hedgerows resemble sloes and some of these are far less acid than the true sloe.

SLOE WINE (Dry)

2 lb. (900 g.) sloes
1 tsp. pectolase
1 gal. (4·5 l.) water
1 Campden tablet or 1 fl. oz. sulphite solution A
3 lb. (1·4 kg.) sugar
1 level tsp. yeast nutrient
Pommard yeast

Make as for Damson Wine (Dry), page 114.

SLOE WINE (Sweet)

3 lb. (1·4 kg.) sloes
1 tsp. pectolase
1 gal. (4·5 l.) water
1 Campden tablet or 1 fl. oz. sulphite solution A
3½ lb. (1·6 kg.) sugar
1 level tsp. yeast nutrient
all purpose yeast
heavy sugar syrup, optional

Make as for Damson Wine (Sweet), page 115.

STRAWBERRIES

Strawberries do not make a good dry wine, but they make a very pleasant sweet one. The best variety to grow at home is Royal Sovereign, one of the oldest varieties; the flavour is unsurpassed by any modern variety. Royal Sovereign is seldom grown commercially as it does not give a large crop. Gather fruit for wine making during a dry, sunny spell, making sure it is sound and fully ripe.

STRAWBERRY WINE (Rosé)

4 lb. (1·8 kg.) strawberries
1 gal. (4·5 l.) water, approx.
1 tsp. pectolase
1½ Campden tablets or 1½ fl. oz. sulphite solution A
3 lb. (1·4 kg.) sugar
½ oz. (15 g.) citric acid
1 level tsp. yeast nutrient
½ level tsp. grape tannin
all purpose yeast
heavy sugar syrup, optional

Wash the strawberries, put them in the fermentation vessel and crush them. Pour over them 4 pt. cold water, and add the pectolase and 1 crushed Campden tablet or 1 fl. oz. sulphite solution. Cover and leave for 24 hours.

Strain the pulp, measure the juice and make it up to 6 pt. with cold water; return the 6 pt. liquor to the strawberry pulp. Heat 2 pt. water and in it dissolve the sugar, acid, yeast nutrient and tannin; cool it to 80°F (27°C) and pour it into the strawberry must. Add an active yeast culture, stir, cover closely and ferment the pulp at 70°F (21°C) for 2 days. Strain the pulp and pour the wine into a clean

1-gal. jar, fit an airlock and ferment at 65°F (18°C). When fermentation stops, rack the wine into a clean jar and store in a cool place. Rack again at regular intervals to stabilise the wine. After 6 months, taste it and sweeten if necessary with heavy sugar syrup, then add the extra ½ crushed Campden tablet or ½ fl. oz. sulphite solution.

STRAWBERRY WINE (Sweet)

5–6 lb. (2·3–2·7 kg.) strawberries
1 gal. (4·5 l.) water, approx.
1 tsp. pectolase
1½ Campden tablets or 1½ fl. oz. sulphite solution A
3 lb. (1·4 kg.) sugar
½ pt. (280 ml.) red grape concentrate
¼ oz. (7 g.) citric acid
1 level tsp. yeast nutrient
½ level tsp. grape tannin
Sauternes yeast
heavy sugar syrup, optional

Prepare the must as for Strawberry Wine (Rosé), above, making the liquor up to 6 pt. after the first 24 hours. Then heat 2 pt. water and in it dissolve 2½ lb. sugar, the grape concentrate, acid, yeast nutrient and tannin. Add this to the must and continue to ferment as for Strawberry Wine (Rosé). Dissolve the remaining ½ lb. sugar in the wine after straining it. Feed the wine with heavy sugar syrup when the gravity drops to 5 (1·005) and add the extra ½ crushed Campden tablet or ½ fl. oz. sulphite solution.

Dried fruit wines

The method for all wines made with dried fruit is the same. Raisins, sultanas, dates and figs all have a high sugar content and it is important to know exactly what this is in order to control the amount of sugar added. Sugar quantities given in recipes are only a rough guide. A mixture of dried fruits may be used, but the total weight should not exceed 3 lb. per gallon.

Method for all dried fruit wines

Chop the fruit and cook it in a pressure cooker at 15 lb. pressure for 15 minutes, or boil it in 3 pt. water until well cooked. Strain the pulp, wash it twice with 1½ pt. water, press the pulp and discard it. Measure the cooking liquor and make it up to 1 gal. (4·5 l.) with cold water. Take a gravity reading of this juice and estimate the amount of sugar required to raise the gravity to 100 (1·100). Heat 2 pt. of the liquor and in it dissolve the calculated amount of sugar and acid, yeast nutrient and tannin as indicated in the recipe. Return this to the bulk. Allow the liquor to cool to 70°F (21°C), then add pectolase, stir briskly to introduce oxygen, then add the active yeast culture.

Divide the must between two clean 1-gal. jars, fit airlocks and ferment at 70°F (21°C). When the first vigorous fermentation subsides, gently fill one jar from the other, re-fit an airlock and ferment on at 65°F (18°C). When fermentation has stopped, rack and store in a cool place. If a sweet wine is required, feed it with heavy sugar syrup when the gravity drops to 5 (1·005).

DATE WINE

2½ lb. (1·2 kg.) dates
1 gal. (4·5 l.) water
1½ lb. (680 g.) sugar, approx.
½ oz. (15 g.) citric acid
1 level tsp. yeast nutrient
1 level tsp. grape tannin
1 tsp. pectolase
sherry yeast
heavy sugar syrup, optional

Make as for Dried Fruit Wine, page 119.

FIG WINE

2 lb. (900 g.) figs
1 gal. (4·5 l.) water
1¾ lb. (780 g.) sugar
½ oz. (15 g.) citric acid
1 level tsp. yeast nutrient
½ level tsp. grape tannin
1 tsp. pectolase
Tokay yeast
heavy sugar syrup, optional

Make as for Dried Fruit Wine, page 119.

SULTANA WINE

3 lb. (1·4 kg.) sultanas
1 gal. (4·5 l.) water
1¼ lb. (560 g.) sugar, approx.
½ oz. (15 g.) citric acid
1 level tsp. yeast nutrient
½ level tsp. grape tannin
1 tsp. pectolase
Tokay yeast
heavy sugar syrup, optional

Make as for Dried Fruit Wine, page 119.

RAISIN WINE (Dry)

2 lb. (900 g.) raisins, soaked overnight and drained
1 gal. (4·5 l.) water
1½ lb. (675 g.) sugar, approx.
½ oz. (15 g.) citric acid
1 level tsp. yeast nutrient
½ level tsp. grape tannin
1 tsp. pectolase
all purpose yeast

Boil the soaked raisins and make as for Dried Fruit Wine, page 119.

RAISIN WINE (Sweet)

2½ lb. (1·2 kg.) raisins
1 gal. (4·5 l.) water
1½ lb. (675 g.) sugar, approx.
½ oz. (15 g.) citric acid
1 level tsp. yeast nutrient
½ level tsp. grape tannin
1 tsp. pectolase
Tokay yeast
heavy sugar syrup, optional

Make as for Dried Fruit Wine, page 119.

Flower wines

Flower wines are light and delicate and, as one might expect from the small quantity of ingredients used, inclined to be thin in body. More body can be introduced by adding either ½ lb. sultanas or ½ pt. grape concentrate. If you use sultanas, chop them and ferment them with the must for 4 days, then strain. If you use grape concentrate, dissolve it in the must with the sugar. In both cases, reduce the amount of sugar indicated in the recipe by 4 oz.

Method for all flower wines

Put the petals in a fermentation vessel and pour 1 gal. boiling water over them. Leave to infuse for 24 hours, then strain. Discard the petals. Add sugar, yeast nutrient, grape tannin and citric acid as indicated in the recipes. Add an active yeast culture and stir the must briskly to introduce oxygen. Divide it between two clean 1-gal. jars, fit airlocks and ferment the wine at 70°C (21°C) until the first, vigorous fermentation subsides. Gently fill one jar from the other, re-fit an airlock and ferment on at 65°F (18°C). Rack and store in a cool place.

ELDERFLOWER WINE (Dry)

¾ pt. (450 ml.) elderflowers, loosely packed
1 gal. (4·5 l.) water
2½ lb. (1·2 kg.) sugar
1 level tsp. yeast nutrient
½ level tsp. grape tannin
½ oz. (15 g.) citric acid
Chablis yeast

Make as for Flower Wines, above.

ELDERFLOWER WINE (Sweet)

1 pt. (580 ml.) elderflowers, loosely packed
1 gal. (4·5 l.) water
3 lb. (1·4 kg.) sugar
1 level tsp. yeast nutrient
½ level tsp. grape tannin
½ oz. (15 g.) citric acid
Sauternes yeast

Make as for Flower Wines, above.

RED ROSE PETAL WINE (Sweet)

4 pt. (2·25 l.) rose petals, loosely packed
1 gal. (4·5 l.) water
3 lb. (1·4 kg.) sugar
1 level tsp. yeast nutrient
½ oz. (15 g.) citric acid
all purpose yeast

Make as for Flower Wines, page 122.

CARNATION PETAL WINE (Dry)

3 pt. (1·7 l.) carnation petals, loosely packed
1 gal. (4·5 l.) water
2½ lb. (1·2 kg.) sugar
1 level tsp. yeast nutrient
½ level tsp. grape tannin
½ oz. (15 g.) citric acid
Chablis yeast

Make as for Flower Wines, page 122.

CARNATION PETAL WINE (Sweet)

4 pt. (2·25 l.) carnation petals, loosely packed
1 gal. (4·5 l.) water
3 lb. (1·4 kg.) sugar
1 level tsp. yeast nutrient
½ level tsp. grape tannin
½ oz. (15 g.) citric acid
Tokay yeast

Make as for Flower Wines, page 122.

COWSLIP WINE (Dry)

6 pt. (3·4 l.) cowslip flowers, loosely packed
1 gal. (4·5 l.) water
2½ lb. (1·2 kg.) sugar
1 level tsp. yeast nutrient
½ level tsp. grape tannin
½ oz. (15 g.) citric acid
Chablis yeast

Make as for Flower Wines, page 122.

COWSLIP WINE (Sweet 1)

1 gal. (4·5 l.) cowslip flowers, loosely packed
1 gal. (4·5 l.) water
3 lb. (1·4 kg.) sugar
1 level tsp. yeast nutrient
½ level tsp. grape tannin
½ oz. (15 g.) citric acid
Tokay yeast

Make as for Flower Wines, page 122.

COWSLIP WINE (Sweet 2)

Ingredients as for Cowslip Wine (Sweet 1).

Heat 3 pt. water and dissolve in it the sugar, yeast nutrient, acid and tannin. Add 5 pt. cold water and stir well. Cool to 70°F (21°C), then add an active yeast culture. Stand this must in a temperature of 70°F (21°C) and when it is fermenting vigorously add the freshly picked cowslips. Ferment the flowers for 4 days, then strain the wine into a clean 1-gal. jar and ferment on at 65°F (18°C). Rack and store in a cool place.

MARIGOLD PETAL WINE (Sweet)

3 pt. (1·2 l.) marigold petals, loosely packed
1 gal. (4·5 l.) water
3 lb. (1·4 kg.) sugar
1 level tsp. yeast nutrient
½ oz. (15 g.) citric acid
Tokay yeast

Make as for Flower Wines, page 122.

Herb wines

Like flower petals, herbs are deficient in acid and yeast nutrient and the wines are improved by the addition of a small quantity of sultanas.

TEA WINE

1 gal. (4·5 l.) water
3 oz. (90 g.) Earl Grey tea
4 oz. (110 g.) sultanas
2½ lb. (1·2 kg.) sugar
¼ oz. (7 g.) citric acid
1 level tsp. yeast nutrient
all purpose yeast
1 tsp. pectolase
heavy sugar syrup, optional

Pour 4 pt. boiling water over the tea and infuse for ½ hour, then strain. Put the chopped sultanas in a pan with 2 pt. water, bring to the boil and dissolve the sugar, acid and yeast nutrient. Pour this into the tea and add another 2 pt. cold water. Allow the must to cool to 70°F (21°C) and add an active yeast culture and the pectolase, stir briskly to introduce oxygen, cover closely and ferment at 70°F (21°C) for 5 days. Strain off the sultanas, pour the wine into a clean 1-gal. jar, fit an airlock and ferment at 65°F (18°C) to dryness. Rack and store in a cool place.

For a sweet wine, feed with heavy sugar syrup when the gravity drops to 5 (1·005).

LEMON BALM WINE (Dry)

4 pt. (2·25 l.) lemon balm tips, loosely packed
1 gal. (4·5 l.) water
2½ lb. (1·2 kg.) sugar
½ oz. (15 g.) citric acid
1 level tsp. yeast nutrient
1 tsp. pectolase
Chablis yeast

Put the balm tips in the fermentation vessel and pour over 6 pt. boiling water. Leave for 24 hours, then strain and discard the herbs. Heat 2 pt. water and dissolve in it the sugar, acid and yeast nutrient. Pour this into the strained liquor. When the must has cooled to 70°F (21°C) add the pectolase and the active yeast culture. Stir briskly, divide the must between two jars, fit airlocks and leave them at 70°F to ferment. Gently fill one jar from the other when the first, vigorous fermentation subsides, re-fit the airlock and ferment at 65°F (18°C) to dryness. Rack and store in a cool place.

LEMON BALM WINE (Sweet)

5 pt. (2·8 l.) lemon balm tips, loosely packed
1 gal. (4·5 l.) water
1 lb. (450 g.) sultanas
2½ lb. (1·2 kg.) sugar
½ oz. (15 g.) citric acid
1 level tsp. yeast nutrient
½ level tsp. grape tannin
1 tsp. pectolase
Tokay yeast
heavy sugar syrup, optional

Put the balm tips in a fermentation vessel and pour over 6 pt. boiling water. Leave for 24 hours, then strain and discard the herbs.

Put 2 pt. water in a pan with the chopped sultanas, bring to the boil and dissolve in it the sugar, acid, yeast nutrient and tannin; add this to the strained balm liquor. When the must has cooled to 70°F (21°C), add the pectolase and the active yeast culture. Stir well, cover closely and ferment at 70°F for 5 days, stirring daily. Strain the wine, pour it into a clean 1-gal. jar, fit an airlock and ferment on at 65°F (18°C). When fermentation has stopped, rack and store in a cool place. Sweeten with heavy sugar if a sweeter wine is required.

PARSLEY WINE (Dry)

¾ lb. (340 g.) parsley
1 gal. (4·5 l.) water
4 oz. (112 g.) sultanas
juice from 4 sweet oranges
2½ lb. (1·2 kg.) sugar
1 level tsp. yeast nutrient
½ oz. (15 g.) citric acid
all purpose yeast
1 tsp. pectolase

Wash the parsley and remove any large stalks as these would make the flavour too pronounced. Put the parsley in a fermentation vessel and pour 1 gal. boiling water over it. Infuse for 24 hours, then strain and discard the herbs.

Bring to the boil 2 pt. of the parsley water, add the chopped sultanas and orange juice and dissolve the sugar, yeast nutrient and acid in it. Return it to the bulk and allow to cool to 70°F (21°C). Add the active yeast culture and pectolase, cover and ferment at 70°F for 4 days. Strain the must, pour the wine into a clean 1-gal. jar, fit an airlock and ferment at 65°F (18°C) to dryness. Rack and store in a cool place

PARSLEY WINE (Sweet)

1 lb. (450 g.) parsley
juice of 5 sweet oranges
1 gal. (4·5 l.) water
½ lb. (225 g.) sultanas
2¾ lb. (1·3 kg.) sugar
1 level tsp. yeast nutrient
½ oz. (15 g.) citric acid
Tokay yeast
1 tsp. pectolase

Make as for Parsley Wine (Dry), page 126.

Grain wines

Dried fruit is used in grain wine recipes to give the wine more flavour and character. The fruit may be varied to suit the individual palate.

RICE WINE (Sweet)

3 lb. (1·4 kg.) patna rice
1 gal. (4·5 l.) water
3 lb. (1·4 kg.) sugar
½ oz. (15 g.) citric acid
1 level tsp. yeast nutrient
1 lb. (450 g.) raisins
Tokay yeast
heavy sugar syrup

Use only high grade polished rice and wash it well under cold running water to remove any starch. Make as for Wheat and Raisin Wine (Sweet), page 128.

After straining the must, throw the mash out in the garden – the birds will love it.

WHEAT AND RAISIN WINE (Sweet)

1 gal. (4·5 l.) water
2½ lb. (1·2 kg.) sugar
½ oz. (15 g.) citric acid
1 level tsp. yeast nutrient
1 lb. (450 g.) wheat
2 lb. (900 g.) raisins
sherry yeast
heavy sugar syrup

Bring all the water to the boil and dissolve in it the sugar, acid and yeast nutrient. Pour this over the wheat and raisins in the fermentation vessel. When the must has cooled to 70°F (21°C), stir briskly and check the temperature again before adding an active yeast culture – there is often residual heat in the ingredients at the bottom of the container that might destroy the yeast. Cover the vessel closely and ferment the pulp for 10 days at 70°F, stirring twice daily. Strain the must and pour the wine into a clean 1-gal. jar, fit an airlock and ferment on at 65°F (18°C). Feed with heavy sugar when the gravity drops to 5 (1·005). Rack and store in a cool place.

Vegetable wines

PARSNIPS

Parsnips may be used for both dry and sweet wines, though the sweet is rather better. To tone down the flavour a little, peel the parsnips before use and do not overcook them; boiling in an open pan will also help.

PARSNIP WINE (Dry)

3 lb. (1·4 kg.) parsnips
1 gal. (4·5 l.) water
2½ lb. (1·2 kg.) sugar
½ oz. (15 g.) citric acid
1 level tsp. grape tannin
1 level tsp. yeast nutrient
1 tsp. pectolase
Chablis yeast

Wash the parsnips and peel them; cut into pieces and boil in an open pan until just tender. Do not overcook them. Strain the vegetables but do not press or squeeze them; set the parsnips aside for eating. Measure the liquor and make it up to 6 pt. with cold water. Heat 2 pt. water and dissolve in it the sugar, acid, tannin and yeast nutrient. Add this to the parsnip liquor and when cooled to 70°F (21°C) add the pectolase and the active yeast culture. Stir briskly, divide the must between two clean 1-gal. jars, fit airlocks and ferment at 70°F until the vigorous fermentation has subsided. Gently fill one jar from the other, re-fit the airlock and ferment at 65°F (18°C) to dryness. Rack and store in a cool place.

PARSNIP WINE (Sweet)

4 lb. (1·8 kg.) parsnips
1 lb. (450 g.) sultanas
1 gal. (4·5 l.) water
3 lb. (1·4 kg.) sugar
½ oz. (15 g.) citric acid
1 level tsp. grape tannin
1 level tsp. yeast nutrient
1 tsp. pectolase
sherry yeast

Prepare the parsnips as for Parsnip Wine (Dry), page 128, chop the sultanas and boil them together. Strain and continue as for Parsnip Wine (Dry), using 2½ lb. sugar initially and dissolving the remainder in the must before filling one jar into the other. This wine will be improved by storing in cask for a year.

CARROTS

CARROT WINE (Sweet)

4 lb. (1·8 kg.) carrots
1 gal. (4·5 l.) water
1 tsp. pectolase
3 lb. (1·4 kg.) sugar
½ oz. (15 g.) citric acid
1 level tsp. yeast nutrient
½ level tsp. grape tannin
all purpose yeast

Scrub the carrots and cut them in pieces. Boil until just tender; do not overcook. Strain but do not press the carrots, measure the liquor and make it up to 6 pt. with cold water. Heat 2 pt. water and in it dissolve the pectolase, sugar, acid, yeast nutrient and tannin; add this to the carrot liquor. When the must has cooled to 70°F (21°C) add the active yeast culture, then proceed as for Parsnip Wine (Sweet).

BEETROOTS

BEETROOT WINE (Sweet)

3 lb. (1·4 kg.) young beetroots
1 gal. (4·5 l.) water
3 lb. (1·4 kg.) sugar
½ oz. (15 g.) citric acid
1 level tsp. yeast nutrient
all purpose yeast

Wash the beetroot well and slice it. Boil in an open pan until tender. Strain but do not press or squeeze. Make as for Parsnip Wine (Sweet), page 129.

MANGOLD WURZEL, OR SUGAR BEET WINE

Use the recipe for Parsnip Wine (Sweet), page 129.

BIRCH SAP

Birch sap is collected in March when the sap is rising. Collect it carefully otherwise the tree will be harmed. Collect sap only from trees with a circumference of about 30–36 inches, and do not collect sap from the same tree in two successive years. Take no more than 1 gal. from any one tree in a year.

Starting about 18 inches above the ground, bore a small hole about $\frac{5}{8}$-in. diameter upwards into the tree to a depth of about $1\frac{1}{2}$ in. Insert a piece of $\frac{5}{8}$-in. diameter tubing into the hole, place a jar at the other end of the tube and seal the opening of the jar with polythene.

When you have a gallon of sap, plug the hole in the tree with a piece of wooden dowelling, driven home tightly with a mallet. Birch sap has very little flavour and it is usual to use either raisins or sultanas with it.

BIRCH SAP WINE (Sweet)

1 gal. (4·5 l.) birch sap
½ lb. (225 g.) raisins
2½ lb. (1·2 kg.) sugar
4 fl. oz. (120 ml.) orange juice
1 level tsp. yeast nutrient
½ oz. (15 g.) citric acid
1 level tsp. grape tannin
all purpose yeast
heavy sugar syrup, optional

Boil together the sap, raisins and sugar for 5 minutes. Allow to cool, then add the orange juice, yeast nutrient, acid and tannin. When the temperature has fallen to 70°F (21°C) add the active yeast culture and stir well. Cover the vessel and ferment at 70°F for 4 days. Strain the must and fill the wine into a clean 1-gal. jar. Fill to approximately ½ in. below the cork, fit an airlock and ferment on at 65°F (18°C). Rack and store in a cool place.

If the wine is too dry when fermentation stops, sweeten with heavy sugar syrup.

Sparkling wines

Make sparkling wines from ingredients that will produce a lightly flavoured wine. Grapes, pears, apples, vine prunings, fresh apricots, peaches, elderflowers and gooseberries are all suitable.

Use a minimum amount of the main ingredient to ensure that the wine is not overflavoured and do not use more than 2 lb. sugar per gallon. Ferment the wine with a Champagne or all purpose yeast. When fermentation stops, measure the gravity with a hydrometer. If the wine is dry, rack it into a clean 1-gal. jar and store in a cool place, then rack at intervals until the wine is perfectly clear. Only then should you rack the wine into the sterilised Champagne bottles. (Sterilise the bottles with sulphite solution B and rinse with cold boiled water until all traces of sulphite are removed.) When filling the bottles, leave about 3 in. air space at the top; pour $\frac{1}{2}$ fl. oz. heavy sugar syrup into each bottle if the wine is quite dry and add a little active yeast starter; the air space will now be about 2 in. Close each bottle with a plastic Champagne stopper, using a wooden mallet to drive it home, and wire the stoppers in position.

Store the bottles for several weeks at a temperature of 65°F (18°C). If the wine is to be disgorged (page 13), store them in an inverted position; if it is to be drunk without disgorgement, store the bottles upright and twist them every 2 months to settle the sediment on the bottom of the bottle. The wine will take about 9 months to reach the right condition for drinking.

Never use bottles other than Champagne bottles; these are the only type strong enough to hold the pressure that builds up in a sparkling wine. Be sure the wine does not contain too much sugar when bottled, or excessive gas will form.

SPARKLING GOOSEBERRY WINE

2 lb. (900 g.) green gooseberries
1 tsp. pectolase
1 gal. (4·5 l.) water
1 Campden tablet or 1 fl. oz. sulphite solution A
2 lb. (900 g.) sugar
1 level tsp. yeast nutrient
Champagne or all purpose yeast

Make as for **Gooseberry Wine (Dry)**, page 98, then rack and bottle as for a sparkling wine.

SPARKLING APPLE WINE

5 pt. (2·8 l.) fresh apple juice
1 Campden tablet or 1 fl. oz. sulphite solution A
3 pt. (1·8 l.) water
sugar, sufficient to raise the gravity to 65 (1·065)
1 level tsp. citric acid
1 level tsp. yeast nutrient
Champagne or all purpose yeast

Make as for Apple Wine (Dry), page 86, then rack and bottle as for a sparkling wine.

SPARKLING APRICOT WINE

2 lb. (900 g.) fresh apricots
1 gal. (4·5 l.) water
2 tsps. pectolase
1 Campden tablet or 1 fl. oz. sulphite solution A
2 lb. (900 g.) sugar
1 level tsp. yeast nutrient
Champagne or all purpose yeast

Make as for Apricot Wine (Dry), page 87, then rack and bottle as for a sparkling wine.

SPARKLING WHITE CURRANT WINE

2 lb. (900 g.) white currants
1 tsp. pectolase
1 gal. (4·5 l.) water
1 Campden tablet or 1 fl. oz. sulphite solution A
2 lb. (900 g.) sugar
1 level tsp. yeast nutrient
Champagne or all purpose yeast

Make as for White Currant Wine (Dry), page 93, then rack and bottle as for sparkling wines.

SPARKLING PEACH WINE

1½ lb. (675 g.) fresh peaches
1 gal. (4·5 l.) water
2 tsps. pectolase
1 level tsp. citric acid
1 Campden tablet or 1 fl. oz. sulphite solution A
2 lb. (900 g.) sugar
1 level tsp. yeast nutrient
Champagne or all purpose yeast

Make as for Peach Wine (Dry), page 110, then rack and store as for sparkling wines.

Port and sherry type wines

PORT TYPE WINE

Commercial port wine is made from black grapes and the fermentation is stopped when about half-way through by the addition of alcohol. We have to use a different method to produce port type wines.

The best fruits to use are blackberries, bilberries, elderberries, damsons or loganberries. The fruits may be mixed but the total quantity should not exceed 4 lb. per gallon of wine. The fruit content of the must should be high, a high alcohol content is desirable and the wine should be matured for a year if possible in cask. The new wine will be harsh, but will mellow on storage.

PORT TYPE WINE

5 lb. (2·2 kg.) blackberries
  or 4 lb. (1·8 kg.) damsons
  or 4 lb. (1·8 kg.) elderberries
  or 4 lb. (1·8 kg.) fresh or bottled bilberries
  or 4 lb. (1·8 kg.) loganberries
1 gal. (4·5 l.) water
2 tsps. pectolase
1 Campden tablet or 1 fl. oz. sulphite solution A
½ pt. (300 ml.) red grape concentrate
3–3½ lb. (1·4–1·6 kg.) sugar
1 level tsp. yeast nutrient
port yeast
heavy sugar syrup
3–5 fl. oz. brandy or vodka, optional

Put the fruit in a fermentation vessel, crush or bruise it and pour over 4 pt. cold water. Add the pectolase and a crushed Campden tablet or the sulphite solution. Cover and leave for 24 hours.

Heat 2 pt. water and in it dissolve the grape concentrate and 1 lb. sugar; when it has cooled to 80°F (27°C), add it to the fruit. Stir well, add the yeast nutrient and an active yeast culture. Ferment the pulp for 3 days, stirring twice daily; if stone fruit is used, remove as many stones as possible after 24 hours, using well scrubbed hands. Press or strain the must. Heat a further 2 pt. water and dissolve in it 1 lb. sugar; cool this to 70°F (21°C) and add to the must. Stir, pour into a clean 1-gal. jar and leave to ferment at 65°F (18°C). Do not be surprised if there is a slight delay in fermentation. Some free oxygen has been introduced into the must and this will induce a further period of yeast growth. When all the free oxygen has been utilised, fermentation will start again. Ferment until the gravity has dropped to 5 (1·005), then feed the wine with heavy sugar syrup, 4 fl. oz. at a time, until fermentation stops. The final gravity of the wine should be between 15 and 20 (1·015–1·020).

When fermentation stops, rack and store the wine in a cool place. It will require 3–4 years storage before it becomes mellow. It can be improved by the addition of 3–5 fl. oz. brandy or vodka, and by a year in cask.

SHERRY TYPE WINE

This is the only wine that is fermented and stored with an air space in the container. With all other wines the greatest care is taken not to expose the wine to air, as air causes oxidation. With sherry type wines this exposure is essential as it helps to impart the characteristic sherry flavour to the wine. A sherry yeast is of course used.

In the commercial production of sherry, a flor, or floating yeast culture is sometimes produced on the surface of the wine. This is called the 'sherry flor'; it will not form at all unless the alcohol content is just right, about 15%, the SO_2 content is below 180 parts per million, the wine is in the right temperature (about 20°C) and the right amount of acid is present. The resulting sherry will be a fino. This is a light coloured wine. If no flor has formed the wine will be much darker, with a heavier flavour and a higher sugar residue.

The main variety of grape used in sherry production is the Palomino grape. The grapes are subjected to special treatment before processing: they are spread on grass mats to dry in the sun, so that their sugar content is greatly increased. The limited resources of the amateur can produce a wine with only some of the sherry characteristics. Nevertheless such wines can be very pleasant and compare favourably with some sherry wines produced in countries other than Spain.

Not all ingredients lend themselves to the production of sherry type wines. The best are oranges and apples for dry wine, wheat and raisins for sweet; parsnips may also be used for dry.

SHERRY TYPE WINE (Dry) 1

4 pt. (2·3 l.) juice from sweet oranges
1 tsp. pectolase
½ oz. (15 g.) citric acid
1 Campden tablet or 1 fl. oz. sulphite solution A
1 level tsp. yeast nutrient
1 lb. (450 g.) sultanas
3 pt. (1·7 l.) water, approx.
2 lb. (900 g.) sugar
sherry yeast

Mix the orange juice, pectolase, acid, sulphite and yeast nutrient in a fermentation vessel. Chop the sultanas and boil them in 3 pt. water for 15 minutes. Strain and discard the sultanas, measure the cooking liquor and make it up to 3 pt. again with cold water. Dissolve the sugar in the liquor, allow it to cool to 80°F (27°C), then add it to the must. Add the active yeast culture, pour it into a clean jar, plug the opening with cotton wool and ferment at 70°F (21°C) for 5 days. Reduce the temperature to 65°F (18°C) and ferment to dryness. Rack the wine, cork the jar this time and store in a cool place.

SHERRY TYPE WINE (Dry) 2

3 lb. (1·4 kg.) parsnips
1 lb. (450 g.) sultanas
1 gal. (4·5 l.) water
2½ lb. (1·2 kg.) sugar
½ oz. (15 g.) citric acid
1 level tsp. yeast nutrient
1 tsp. pectolase
sherry yeast
6 fl. oz. brandy or other spirit, optional

Wash, peel and cut up the parsnips and boil them in an open pan with the chopped sultanas until just tender. Then continue as for Parsnip Wine (Dry), page 128. Do not fill the jars more than seven-eighths full for fermentation, and plug the opening with cotton wool.

When the wine has finished fermenting, rack it and store in a container again filled only seven-eighths full. This time close the container with a cork. Sherry type wine is best stored in a cask and is also greatly improved by the addition of 6 fl. oz. brandy or other spirit for each gallon. The extra alcohol also acts as a safeguard against infection.

SHERRY TYPE WINE (Sweet) 1

1 lb. (450 g.) raisins
5 pt. (2·8 l.) fresh apple juice
1 tsp. pectolase
1 level tsp. citric acid
1 Campden tablet or 1 fl. oz. sulphite solution A
2 pt. (1·1 l.) water
2½ lb. (1·2 kg.) sugar
1 pt. (0·57 l.) white grape concentrate
1 level tsp. yeast nutrient
sherry yeast
heavy sugar syrup

Chop the raisins into small pieces and put them in a fermentation vessel. Add the apple juice, pectolase, acid and a crushed Campden tablet or the sulphite solution. Cover and leave for 24 hours.

Heat 2 pt. water and in it dissolve 2 lb. sugar, the grape concentrate and yeast nutrient. Allow it to cool to 80°F (27°C) and add to the apple juice. Next add the active yeast culture, cover the vessel and ferment the pulp for 6 days at 70°F (21°C), stirring twice daily. Strain the must and dissolve ½ lb. sugar in the juice. Pour it into a clean 1-gal. jar, filling it only seven-eighths full, and plug the neck with cotton wool. Ferment on at 65°F (18°C). Feed the wine with sugar syrup when the gravity drops to 5 (1·005). Rack and store in a cool place, with the container corked.

SHERRY TYPE WINE (Sweet) 2

2 lb. (900 g.) wheat
2 lb. (900 g.) raisins
7 pt. (4 l.) water
2½ lb. (1·2 kg.) sugar
½ oz. (15 g.) citric acid
1 level tsp. yeast nutrient
1 tsp. pectolase
sherry yeast
heavy sugar syrup

Put the wheat and chopped raisins into a fermentation vessel. Boil 7 pt. water and dissolve in it 2 lb. sugar, the acid and yeast nutrient. Pour this over the wheat and raisins. Cool to 70°F (21°C) then add the pectolase and an active yeast culture. Cover the vessel and ferment the pulp at 70°F for 10 days, stirring twice daily. Strain the must and dissolve ½ lb. sugar in the liquor, pour it into a clean jar, leaving an airspace, and plug the neck with cotton wool. Ferment on at 65°F (18°C). When the gravity drops to 5 (1·005), feed with sugar syrup. When fermentation stops, rack and store the wine in a corked container in a cool place.

12

Beer

There are many kinds of English beer, each with its own characteristic. The lighter, or lower alcohol beers are the light ales and light bitters. Next we have the popular best bitters and Burton type bitters. Of the darker beers the brown ales vary from the sweet London browns to Newcastle brown, which is lighter in colour but heavier in alcohol. There are also sweet and dry stouts. The last British beer, and considered by many to be the best, is barley wine. This is an extremely strong beer, which is brewed, bottled and left for two years to mature.

Malt

The ingredients needed to make all these beers are basically malt, hops, sugars, yeast and water. Malt is roasted barley. Light malt is the lightest roasted, and is used in all beers in conjunction with darker malts to produce certain types of beer. Slightly darker in colour is crystal malt, followed by brown, chocolate, and finally black malt. It must be remembered that the darker the colour of the malt, the less fermentable the substance but the more flavour it contains. The malt used by many amateurs is malt extract. This is obtainable in the form of dry malt, which looks like brown sugar, or as a thick syrup-like substance.

Adjuncts

Some unmalted materials such as flaked maize, flaked rice, brumore and wheat syrup are used to add body to a beer and cut down brewing costs; these are known as adjuncts.

Caragheen (Irish) moss can be used to help produce bright beers. This is obtainable from any good wine and beer stockist, and is very simple to use. Just add the required amount to the wort during boiling. It can be used in all recipes.

Hops come in many varieties. English hops are male hops, that is seeded. The amateur should know the different varieties, since they confer a particular characteristic to his brews. Fuggles, Whitbread Golding Variety, Canterbury Whitebines and Bramling Cross have a normal bittering quality, but for those beer makers who like an extra bitter beer, Northern Brewer or Bullion are hops with a high alpha rate. The latter should be blended with one of the standard varieties until you arrive at a blend suited to your own palate.

Sugar is obtained in many forms. The ordinary granulated sugar obtained from the grocer is quite suitable for beer making, but quality varies and cane sugar is superior to beet sugar. Breweries use an inverted cane sugar for brewing. Light soft brown sugar and Demerara are ideal.

Yeasts used are of two strains, top or bottom working yeasts. Top working yeasts are mainly used for brown ales and certain bitters, while bottom working yeasts are used extensively for best bitters, stouts, lagers and barley wines. It is helpful for the beginner to concentrate on using a bottom working yeast called Sacc. Carlsbergensis. This yeast settles readily and forms a solid sediment on the bottom of the bottle which helps in the pouring of a star bright beer.

Brewers' yeasts are readily obtainable from suppliers of wine and beer equipment, but should you have to resort to using bakers' yeast, rack the beer several times during fermentation. This will mean that you get a minimum of yeast cells at the bottling stage, ensuring a beer free from yeast autolysis or yeast spoilage. Do try to avoid bakers' yeast if at all possible.

Water is a very important factor in brewing. One cannot stress too heavily the influence it has in producing the many characteristics in our beers. Water varies from district to district, from very hard water to extremely soft. For light ales, bitter beers, and barley wines, HARD water should be used. In the production of brown ales and stouts, SOFT water is necessary. Lager should always be brewed with VERY SOFT water.

Equipment

As for winemaking, no special equipment is necessary. Basically, you need a container to heat the various ingredients, such as a large saucepan or better still a preserving pan which will hold approximately 2 gallons. For the fermentation, a polythene dustbin with a lock-on lid is ideal, or a five to ten gallon white container which has been made for fermentation purposes. Whatever plastic container is used, remember that it should be made of high density polythene; this will prevent the beer acquiring a plastic flavour. Your other winemaking equipment such as spoons, syphon tubes etc, will all be pressed into service. Should the water in your area be soft, then you will require the following water hardening agent.

HARDENING AGENT
2 parts gypsum
2 parts common salt
1 part Epsom salts
This should be used in the proportion $\frac{1}{2}$ fl. oz. to 5 gallons water.

Sweetener
A small bottle of liquid saccharin (Sweetex) will come in handy to adjust the sweetness of brown ales and sweet stouts. It is an unfermentable substance and can be used with comparative ease and safety.

Bottling
Only beer or cider bottles should be used, as they alone are made to withstand the gas pressure built up during maturing. Screw-topped or crown corked bottles are the types to look for. Disposable soft drink bottles should not be used, as they are lightweight bottles and made to withstand a KNOWN gas pressure; home brewed beers usually attain a much higher pressure.

Wash the bottles thoroughly in hot water. If screw-topped bottles are being used, remove the rubber washers and wash these. After draining, pour some sulphite solution B into the first bottle, swill around, and pour it into the second bottle. Carry on until all bottles have been treated. Put the washers and stoppers into a container and pour some of the solution over them. On no account wash again with water as the small amount of sulphite will ward off any bacterial infection. At this stage the bottle will smell pungent, but this will disperse by the time the beer reaches maturity.

Having ensured that the bottles are clean, place a syphon tube into the fermentation vessel and gently syphon the beer into the bottles. Prime each bottle with 1 level tsp. sugar and put the cap in position. It is of the utmost importance that $\frac{3}{4}$–1 in. air space is left between the top of the beer and bottom of the closure. This space allows the gas to expand and eliminates any chance of a burst bottle. The bottled beer should be stored in a cool place at 58°F (15°C) in an upright position.

The time taken for maturing will depend on the gravity of the beer. As a rough guide, a light ale should be kept for about 3 weeks before opening, whilst a barley wine should be left for 18 months or more.

Lager

The production of lager is completely different from that of English beers. Lager is made by a system known as decoction, whereas English beers use the infusion method. This means that in lager production more than one temperature is used during the mashing process. There are also other distinctions which help to make lager such an individual beer.

The following material differences are needed to make lager. The water used should be extremely soft (boiled rain water could be used). After boiling, cool, then agitate briskly to introduce oxygen into the water. This is essential for good yeast growth. The malt should be a lager malt, which is malted lighter than pale malt. The hops should be of the continental seedless variety. The fermentation should proceed at a temperature of 43°F (6°C) to allow the full taste to develop.

Beer recipes

LIGHT ALE 1 (Using malt extract)

10 oz. (280 g.) Demerara sugar
3 oz. (84 g.) soft brown sugar
$\frac{1}{2}$ lb. (225 g.) malt extract
$\frac{1}{2}$ tsp. hardening mixture (page 139)
1 gal. (4·5 l.) water
$\frac{1}{2}$ oz. (15 g.) hops (Golding or Fuggles)
beer yeast

Add the sugars, malt extract and hardening mixture to 1 gal. water and bring to the boil, stirring continuously. Add the hops and boil for 20 minutes, keeping the container covered if possible. Strain and cool rapidly. When the temperature has fallen to 60°F (15°C), add the active yeast culture and cover. Some hours later, fermentation will start and a foam will appear on top of the wort. Skim this off and replace the lid of the container. On the second day, when fermentation has settled down, rack the wort into a sterilised 1-gal. jar, fit an airlock and continue the fermentation at 60°F. When the liquid in the airlock has almost ceased to bubble and the top of the beer starts to clear, bottling can start. If testing with a hydrometer, prime and bottle when the gravity is between nil and 4 (1·000–1·004).

LIGHT ALE 2 (Using grain and adjuncts)

1¼ lb. (560 g.) pale malt
2 oz. (56 g.) crystal malt
1 gal. (4·5 l.) water
4 oz. (112 g.) wheat syrup
4 oz. (112 g.) sugar
½–¾ oz. (15–20 g.) hops
½ tsp. hardening mixture (page 139)
beer yeast

Crush the grains and add to the water together with the wheat syrup. Heat to a temperature of 145–150°F (62–65°C) and maintain this temperature until the starch end point is reached.

To check if starch is still present, put a drop of wort into a white saucer and put 1 drop of iodine on to it. If starch is still present the wort will change colour to blue; if the conversion is complete the iodine will remain yellow. Continue mashing (simmering at the given temperature) the grains until this yellow colour indicates that the end point has been reached.

Dissolve the sugar in the wort, add the hops and hardening mixture and boil gently for 30 minutes. Cool the wort quickly to 60°F (15°C) and add the yeast. Ferment out, prime and bottle as for Light Ale 1, above.

BEST BITTER (Using malt extract)

1 gal. (4·5 l.) water
10 oz. (280 g.) malt extract
12 oz. (340 g.) Demerara sugar
6 oz. (170 g.) soft brown sugar
½ tsp. hardening mixture (page 139)
1 oz. (28 g.) hops (½ oz. Fuggles and ½ oz. Bullion)
beer yeast

Bring the water, malt extract, sugars and hardening mixture to the boil, stirring continuously to dissolve them. Add the hops and continue to boil for 20 minutes. Cool the wort to 60°F (15°C) and add the yeast. Ferment out, prime and bottle as for previous recipes. Keep for at least 3 weeks before opening.

SPECIAL I.P.A. (Using grain and adjuncts)

1 gal. (4·5 l.) water
½ tsp. hardening mixture (page 139)
6½ oz. (185 g.) Edme D.M.S. malt extract
1½ oz. (40 g.) flaked wheat
2 oz. (56 g.) flaked rice
7 oz. (200 g.) pale malt
3 oz. (90 g.) crystal malt
1 oz. (28 g.) Styrian hops
½ oz. (14 g.) Golding hops
1 tsp. caragheen moss
5 oz. (140 g.) invert cane sugar
beer yeast

Boil the water and hardening mixture in a closed container for 45 minutes. Allow the temperature to drop to 150°F (65°C), add the malt extract and crushed grains and maintain the temperature until the starch end point is reached (see Light Ale 2, page 141). Add the hops, sugar and caragheen moss and boil for 50 minutes. Cool to 65°F (18°C), syphon off the wort into a clean 1-gal. jar and add the yeast. Any loss of liquid during boiling should be made up with cold water. Fit an airlock and ferment out, prime and bottle as for previous recipes.

BROWN ALE 1 (Using malt extract)

1 gal. (4·5 l.) water
1½ pt. (850 ml.) Munton and Fison malt extract
1 lb. (450 g.) sucrose caramel
1 lb. (450 g.) Demerara sugar
1 oz. (28 g.) Whitbread Golding hops
Grey Owl ale yeast
saccharin

Heat 1 gal. water, add the malt extract, caramel and sugar and simmer, stirring, until dissolved. Add the hops and simmer for a further 30 minutes. Cool the wort rapidly and strain it into a fermentation vessel. Make it up to 1 gal. again with cold water, add the yeast and ferment out as for previous recipes. Before bottling, taste the beer and adjust the sweetness with saccharin (4 drops liquid saccharin are equivalent to 1 tsp. sugar). Prime and bottle in the usual way.

BROWN ALE 2 (Using grain and adjuncts)

12 oz. (340 g.) pale malt
2 oz. (56 g.) crystal malt
1 gal. (4·5 l.) water
2 oz. (56 g.) porridge oats
2 oz. (56 g.) wheat syrup
10 oz. (280 g.) Demerara sugar
6 oz. (170 g.) soft brown sugar
¾ oz. (20 g.) hops
Grey Owl ale yeast
saccharin

Crush the grains and add to the water with the wheat syrup and porridge oats, heat to 138°F (59°C) and maintain this temperature until the starch end point is reached (see Light Ale 2, page 141). Add the sugars and stir until dissolved. Add the hops and simmer for 30 minutes. Cool the wort rapidly, add the yeast and ferment out. Adjust the sweetness with saccharin, prime and bottle.

DRY STOUT 1 (Using malt extract)

1 gal. (4·5 l.) water
8 oz. (225 g.) malt extract
12 oz. (340 g.) soft brown sugar
4 oz. (112 g.) silcose caramel
1 oz. (28 g.) Golding hops
½ oz. (14 g.) Northern Brewer or Bullion hops
beer or lager yeast

Heat the water and add the malt extract, sugar and silcose caramel. Stir until dissolved. Add the blended hops and simmer for 30 minutes. Cool the wort rapidly, add yeast and ferment out. Prime and bottle.

DRY STOUT 2 (Using grain and adjuncts)

1½ lb. (675 g.) pale malt
3 oz. (90 g.) crystal malt
1 oz. (28 g.) black malt
2½ oz. (70 g.) wheat malt
1 gal. (4·5 l.) water
½ oz. (14 g.) Fuggles or Golding hops
½ oz. (14 g.) Bullion or Northern Brewer hops
beer or lager yeast

Crush the grains and add them to the water. Heat to 145–150°F (62–65°C) and maintain this temperature until the starch end point is reached (see Light Ale 2, page 141). Strain off the liquid and make it up to 1 gal. again by washing the residue with water heated to 170°F (75°C); this is known as sparging and washes any residual sugar from the grain; while sparging, pour the water very carefully to avoid binding the grains together. Add the blended hops to the wort and simmer for 30 minutes. Cool rapidly, add the yeast, ferment out, prime and bottle. Keep for 6 weeks before using.

SWEET STOUT

12 oz. (340 g.) pale malt
2 oz. (56 g.) crystal malt
1 gal. (4·5 l.) water
1½ oz. (40 g.) porridge oats
2 oz. (56 g.) Lambert's silcose caramel
½ oz. (14 g.) Fuggles hops
saccharin
beer yeast

Crush the grains, add them to the water with the porridge oats and heat to 138°F (59°C). Maintain this temperature until the starch end point is reached (see Light Ale 2, page 141). Strain and sparge as for Dry Stout 2 (above). Dissolve the silcose caramel in the wort, add the hops and simmer for 30 minutes. Strain, cool rapidly, adjust the sweetness with saccharin, add the yeast and ferment out. Prime, bottle and keep for 3 weeks before using.

BARLEY WINE

1 gal. (4·5 l.) water
1¾ lb. (780 g.) pale malt
3 oz. (90 g.) flaked maize
¾ oz. (20 g.) black malt
1 oz. (28 g.) hops
½ tsp. hardening mixture (page 139)
1½ lb. (675 g.) glucose
yeast
yeast nutrient, optional

Heat the water to 154°F (68°C), add the crushed malt grain and flaked maize and maintain temperatures until the starch end point is reached. Strain and sparge (see Dry Stout 2). Add the hops and hardening mixture and boil for 40 minutes. Strain the wort, add the glucose and stir to dissolve it. Cool rapidly, add yeast and ferment out. As this beer has a high gravity, it may be necessary to stimulate yeast activity with a little yeast nutrient. Prime and bottle in 6-fl. oz. or ½-pt. bottles and store for at least 18 months before drinking.

HEAVY LAGER

1¾ lb. (780 g.) lager malt
½ oz. (14 g.) crystal malt
1 gal. (4·5 l.) water
5 oz. (140 g.) brumore
1 oz. (28 g.) Saaz or Styrian hops
10 oz. (280 g.) white cane sugar
Vierka lager yeast

Crush the grain, add to the water with the brumore and heat to 142–145°F (61–62°C). Maintain temperature for 2 hours. Drop the temperature to 130–132°F (54–55·5°C), maintain the lower temperature for a further 2 hours, then raise the temperature to 150–153°F (56–67°C) and maintain until the starch conversion is complete (see Light Ale 2, page 141). Strain the wort and sparge (see Dry Stout 2, page 144). Add the hops and boil the wort vigorously for 45 minutes. Dissolve the sugar in the wort, make up to 1 gal. with cold water, cool rapidly and add the yeast. Ferment at 43°F (6°C), or as near to this temperature as possible. Prime, bottle and store for at least 8–10 weeks before drinking.

13

Mead

Mead is a fermented drink made from honey, and its history is at least as long as that of wine.

Honey
In order to make the different types of mead successfully, it is necessary to use the right type of honey. The mead maker, to produce a first class mead, must select honey for quality, purity and flavour. As with making wine from fruit, the higher the quality and the better the condition of the ingredient, the higher the quality of the finished product will be. Extracted honey falls into three colour classifications; light, medium and dark. Generally speaking, the flavour of light honey is more delicate than that of medium, with the darkest honey usually being the strongest flavoured. Heather honey is one of the darkest and most strongly flavoured and its use in mead making should be confined to heavy sack meads.

Dry table meads are usually made with the lightest available honey; the sweeter, more robust meads can be made with medium or dark honey. Light honey can also be used for a sweet mead, but dark honey should never be used for a dry mead. English honey is considered the best in the world, as the nectar gathered by the bees comes from a wide variety of flowers both wild and cultivated and this undoubtedly plays an important part in giving the honey its fine flavour. Clover, bean sanfoil, sycamore, apple and lime all make a good dry mead. Charlock honey, although pleasant and mild flavoured when unfermented, should not be used for mead making as it imparts an unpleasant flavour to mead. Blackberry, willow, hawthorn and dandelion honeys all have a stronger flavour, and are best suited to sweet meads.

Honey contains approximately 77% invert sugar and 2% sucrose. It also contains about 17% water. The remaining 4% is made up of acids, dextrins, gums, trace elements of minerals, oils, fats, yeasts, enzymes and flavouring substances. These amounts can vary slightly in different types of honey.

Honey is extracted from the beehive by centrifugal force. First the wax cappings are removed from the combs, then the frames of the comb are spun in a honey extractor which forces the honey from the cells. The honey drains to the bottom of the extractor and is removed by a tap. The honey at this point is liquid but after storage, if the honey is ripe, it will set hard and is then known as granulated honey. Either liquid or granulated honey can be used for mead making.

The cappings from the comb are left to drain. Some beekeepers still use the washings of cappings for mead making but if washings are to be used, it is advisable to wash them as soon as possible and sulphite the honey water with 1 Campden tablet or 1 fl. oz. sulphite solution A to kill the wild yeasts. Honey is then added to raise the gravity. Honey which has started to ferment by itself can be used, but the flavour of the mead will suffer on account of the wild yeast fermentation. There is also a danger that acetic acid has already been formed. Some of this will be dispersed during subsequent fermentation, but some will always remain in the mead. As a rule, mead made from capping washings will seldom have the quality of one made from good quality honey.

As a guide for the average gravity reading of honey when added to one gallon of water, the following table may be useful.

HONEY	GRAVITY
1 lb.	30 (1.030)
1½ lb.	45 (1.045)
2 lb.	60 (1.060)
2½ lb.	75 (1.075)
3 lb.	86 (1.086)
3½ lb.	99 (1.099)
4 lb.	110 (1.110)
4½ lb.	120 (1.120)
5 lb.	129 (1.129)

Acidity

Honey contains about 1% of various acids. These consist mainly of citric and malic acids, but there are traces of formic, succinic and acetic acids.

With this very low acid content it is obvious that more acid needs to be added to the mead must to ensure an efficient fermentation and a well balanced mead. Lack of acid leads to unpleasant medicinal flavours and bitterness, the mead will be flat, 'flabby' and lacking in character; it will also be a prey to spoilage organisms. Quite large amounts of acid are therefore among the normal mead ingredients. Use citric acid rather than lemon juice, as the acid content of lemon juice is variable. It is important to remember that when 3 or 4 lb. honey are diluted with 1 gallon water, all the components of the honey are equally diluted.

Yeast nutrient
Although there are trace elements of yeast nutrient in honey, they are insufficient to meet the demands of the yeast, if it is to reproduce itself sufficiently and ensure a good fermentation. For this reason it is essential to add yeast nutrient to the must; it also helps to add half of a 3 mg. tablet of vitamin B[1] to each gallon of must.

Tannin
Honey is deficient in tannin. The addition of 1 heaped tsp. grape tannin for each gallon of must will improve the flavour and assist clarification of the mead.

Yeasts
Although honey contains a great number of yeasts, it is not advisable to let these conduct the fermentation. They are predominantly wild yeasts and will introduce 'off' flavours and make the mead difficult to clear. They will also produce small amounts of acetic acid which will give the mead a vinegary tang. Instead, the honey and water should first be sterilised and then inoculated with a good sedimentary wine yeast.

For dry meads, a Chablis or all purpose yeast can be used; for a sweet mead, a Sauternes or all purpose yeast. A red melomel (made from a fruit must sweetened with honey) should be fermented with a Pommard yeast to obtain maximum colour extraction from the fruit. For dry white melomels, use a Chablis or Riesling yeast, and for sweet white melomels a Sauternes or Tokay yeast. Alternatively, an all purpose yeast can be used in all cases. The yeast should always be activated before it is added to the must. Prepare a yeast starter as follows.

Yeast starter
Sterilise the bottle for the starter with sulphite solution B and then rinse

several times with boiled water to remove all traces of sulphite. Plug the mouth with cotton wool. Sweeten 4 fl. oz. freshly strained orange juice with ½ oz. sugar, bring this to the boil in a closed pan, then cool to 70°F (21°C), and pour into the starter bottle. Add the yeast culture and re-insert the cotton wool plug. Put the starter in a warm place and it will be ready for use in 2–3 days.

Preparing the must
First decide which type of mead you wish to make and then select the ingredients. Select the honey carefully; many varieties of foreign honey are available; some equipment suppliers sell foreign honey in bulk, making this the most economical way to buy honey if English varieties are too expensive. Canadian clover honey is suitable for dry mead, also some Australian honey, but take care not to use any eucalyptus honey. Although eucalyptus honey is very pleasant, mead made from it has an unpleasant smell and tastes like cough medicine.

As honey contains wild yeasts and other organisms which are detrimental to mead, it must be sterilised. Honey also contains wax particles and pollens, the presence of which will make the mead difficult to clear. To achieve sterilisation and remove these substances, therefore, heat the honey and water to 150°F (65°C) and skim off any scum which forms on the surface. Then add the acid, yeast nutrient and tannin and when the must has cooled to 70°F (21°C), incorporate the active yeast culture. Ferment the mead in a jar fitted with an airlock. The jar should stand in a warm place (70°F) until fermentation has finished.

A dry mead which is intended for table use should not contain too much alcohol, between 10% and 12% v/v. It should be made only from honey and water, unless it is a melomel. Dry mead not intended for table use may have raisins or sultanas added, though additional ingredients are not allowed for competition purposes. For sweet or sack mead production, more honey is used and the alcohol content is therefore higher, 14% v/v or more. Dried fruit and other ingredients may be added, but again not if the mead is intended for show purposes.

Types of mead
Both grape and apple juice can be fermented with honey to produce traditional meads. Other meads have spices added.

PYMENT

Grape juice and honey are fermented together to make a mead called pyment. The traditional pyment was made by adding honey to wine, probably to disguise a harsh wine and make it more palatable.

HIPPOCRAS

Hippocras is a spiced pyment. It is made by suspending a muslin bag containing spices and herbs in the finished pyment. Very little spice should be used or the flavour will be too pronounced. The spices used are largely a matter of personal preference, as are the herbs; they could include tarragon, marjoram, lemon balm, rue, rosemary, aniseed, mace, cinnamon, ginger, lemon or orange peel.

CYSER

Apple juice is fermented with honey to produce cyser. The juice of dessert apples makes good cyser provided the apples can be gathered and processed straight from the tree. A mixture of dessert and cooking apples can also be used, but it is not advisable to use only cooking apples as the mead would tend to be hard and acidic.

MELOMEL

Any fruit juice or pulp, other than grape or apple, fermented with honey is called melomel, for example gooseberry melomel. When making melomels from ingredients with strong flavours, such as mulberries and blackcurrants, and ingredients with a high tannin content, such as elderberries and bilberries, it is better to use either light or medium honey otherwise the honey flavour and fruit extract will be incompatible.

Delicately flavoured ingredients like tangerines or gooseberries should be sweetened with a mild flavoured honey. Heather honey should not be used for melomel because of its overpoweringly strong flavour.

SACK METHEGLIN

Sack metheglin is made by suspending spices in sweet mead.

Mead recipes
MEAD (Dry)

3½ lb. (1·6 kg.) light honey
1 gal. (4·5 l.) water
1 level tsp. grape tannin
½ oz. (15 g.) citric acid
1 level tsp. yeast nutrient
all purpose yeast

Heat the honey and water to 150°F (65°C) and remove any scum that forms on the surface. Add the tannin, acid and yeast nutrient. Cool the liquor to 70°F (21°C) and add the active yeast culture. Stir well. Pour the must into a clean 1-gal. jar, but fill it only seven-eighths full. Pour the remainder into a second jar and fit airlocks to both. Ferment at 70°F until the first vigorous fermentation subsides, then fill the first jar from the second, leaving ½ in. air space between the surface of the mead and the bottom of the cork. Re-fit the airlock and ferment on at 65°F (18°C) to dryness. Rack and store in a cool place.

MEAD, SWEET (Sack mead)

4–5 lb. (1·8–2·3 kg.) medium or dark honey
1 gal. (4·5 l.) water
1 level tsp. grape tannin
½ oz. (15 g.) citric acid
1 level tsp. yeast nutrient
all purpose yeast

Make as for Mead (Dry), above, using 3 lb. honey initially. When the gravity drops to about 5 (1·005), heat 1 lb. honey to 150°F (65°C). Remove about 1 pt. mead from the jar and dissolve half the honey in ½ pt. mead; return this to the jar. Top up with some of the remaining unsweetened mead. Repeat this when the gravity again drops to 5. If the yeasts ferment the second addition of honey, heat yet more honey and repeat the process but add only 4 oz. honey at a time until fermentation stops. Final addition of honey will determine the residual sweetness.

Raisins or sultanas may be added to sack mead if desired. Raisins will confer more flavour to the mead than sultanas. In either case, the sugar content of the fruit must be taken into consideration; deduct half the weight of the fruit added from the amount of honey given in the recipe for sweet mead.

PYMENT

1½ lb. (675 g.) light honey
1 gal. (4·5 l.) fresh grape juice
1 Campden tablet or 1 fl. oz. sulphite solution A
all purpose yeast

Dissolve the honey in the grape juice and add a crushed Campden tablet or 1 fl. oz. sulphite solution. Leave for 24 hours. Add an active yeast culture and continue as as for Mead (Dry), page 151.

CYSER

5 pt. (2·8 l.) fresh apple juice
3 pt. (1·7 l.) water
1 Campden tablet or 1 fl. oz. sulphite solution A
3 lb. (1·4 kg.) honey, approx.
½ oz. (15 g.) citric acid
1 tsp. pectolase
Chablis or all purpose yeast

Mix the apple juice and water and add 1 crushed Campden tablet or the sulphite solution. Leave for 24 hours.

Take a gravity reading and, using the table on page 147, estimate the amount of honey needed to raise the gravity to 100 (1·100). Heat 2 pt. of the apple juice mixture and the required amount of honey to 150°F (65°C), removing any scum that forms on the surface. Add the acid and return to the bulk of the must. When it has cooled to 70°F (21°C) add the pectolase and an active yeast culture. Stir well and continue as for Mead (Dry), page 151.

CYSER (Sweet)

5 pt. (2·8 l.) fresh apple juice
3 pt. (1·7 l.) water
1 Campden tablet or 1 fl. oz. sulphite solution A
4–5 lb. (1·8–2·3 kg.) honey, approx.
½ oz. (15 g.) citric acid
1 level tsp. grape tannin
1 level tsp. yeast nutrient
1 tsp. pectolase
Tokay or all purpose yeast

Mix the apple juice and water and add a crushed Campden tablet or the sulphite solution. Leave for 24 hours.

Take a gravity reading of the juice and, using the table on page 147, estimate the amount of honey required to raise the gravity to 100 (1·100). Heat 2 pt. of the apple juice mixture and the required amount of honey to 150°F (65°C), removing any scum that forms on the surface. Add the acid, tannin and yeast nutrient and return to the bulk of the must. Continue as for Cyser (above).

When the gravity of the cyser drops to 5, feed with honey as for Mead (Sweet), page 151.

CYSER (Sparkling)

4 pt. (2·3 l.) fresh apple juice
4 pt. (2·3 l.) water
1 tsp. pectolase
1 Campden tablet or 1 fl. oz. sulphite solution A
2 lb. (900 g.) light honey
1 level tsp. citric acid, optional
1 level tsp. grape tannin
1 level tsp. yeast nutrient
all purpose yeast
3 fl. oz. (90 ml.) heavy sugar syrup

Mix the apple juice with 2 pt. water, add the pectolase and a crushed Campden tablet or the sulphite solution. Cover and leave for 24 hours.

Heat the honey with 2 pt. water to 150°F (65°C) and remove any scum. When it has cooled to 80°F (27°C), add grape tannin, yeast nutrient and acid if using dessert apples (juice from cooking apples will need no extra acid). Pour into the apple juice. Stir well and add an active yeast culture.

Pour the must into a 1-gal. jar but do not fill more than seven-eighths full; put the remainder into a second jar, fit airlocks and ferment both jars at 70°F (21°C). When the vigorous fermentation subsides, fill the first jar from the second until the surface of the mead is about ½ in. from the bottom of the cork. Re-fit the airlock and ferment at 65°F (18°C) to dryness. Rack and store in a cool place.

Rack at intervals until the cyser is clear, then bring it back into a warm place. Remove a little mead from the jar, add 3 fl. oz. heavy sugar syrup and a little yeast from the starter bottle. Keep the jar in a warm place and as soon as the mead shows signs of fermentation, rack into clean Champagne bottles, leaving 2 in. airspace in each bottle. Fit plastic Champagne stoppers and secure with wires. Store upright at 65°F (18°C) for 2 months, then store in a cool place. Sparkling cyser may be drunk about 9 months after bottling, but will improve if left for a year. When the bottle is opened, pour at once to prevent the sediment from rising.

ORANGE MELOMEL (Dry)

15 oranges
1 gal. (4·5 l.) water, approx.
1 tsp. pectolase
1 Campden tablet or 1 fl. oz. sulphite solution A
3 lb. (1·4 kg.) light honey
½ oz. (15 g.) citric acid
1 level tsp. grape tannin
1 level tsp. yeast nutrient
Chablis or all purpose yeast

Cut the oranges in half and press out the juice, using a lemon squeezer. Discard the pips but retain any pulp particles in the juice. Measure the juice and make it up to 6 pt. with cold water. Pour it into the fermentation vessel, add the pectolase and the pared rind of 3 of the oranges, free of all white pith. Stir in a crushed Campden tablet or the sulphite solution, cover and leave for 24 hours.

Heat the honey with 2 pt. water to 150°F (65°C), removing any scum that forms. Cool to 80°F (27°C) and add the acid, tannin and yeast nutrient. Pour into the orange must and stir well. Add the active yeast culture, cover the vessel closely and ferment at 70°F (21°C) for 4 days. Strain the must, pour the melomel into a clean 1-gal. jar, fit an airlock and ferment at 65°F (18°C) to dryness. Rack and store in a cool place.

PEACH MELOMEL (Dry)

As the flavour of peaches is very light, use only the mildest honey.

2 lb. (900 g.) fresh ripe peaches
1 tsp. pectolase
1 Campden tablet or 1 fl. oz. sulphite solution A
7 pt. (4 l.) water
3 lb. (1·4 kg.) light, mild honey
½ oz. (15 g.) citric acid
1 level tsp. grape tannin
1 level tsp. yeast nutrient
all purpose yeast

Peal the peaches and remove the stones. Cut them into small pieces and put in a fermentation vessel with the pectolase, a crushed Campden tablet or the sulphite solution and 5 pt. cold water. Cover and leave for 24 hours.

Heat the honey and 2 pt. water to 150°F (65°C) and remove any scum. Cool to 80°F (27°C) then add the acid, tannin and yeast nutrient. Pour this over the peaches. Stir well and add the active yeast culture. Cover the vessel closely and ferment the pulp at 70°F (21°C) for 3 days. Strain the must and pour it into a clean 1-gal. jar, fit an airlock and ferment at 65°F (18°C) to dryness. Rack and store in a cool place.

PEACH MELOMEL (Sweet)

3 lb. (1·4 kg.) fresh ripe peaches
1 tsp. pectolase
1 Campden tablet or 1 fl. oz. sulphite solution A
7 pt. (4 l.) water
4–5 lb. (1·8–2·3 kg.) light, mild honey
½ oz. (15 g.) citric acid
1 level tsp. grape tannin
1 level tsp. yeast nutrient
Sauternes or all purpose yeast

Make as for Peach Melomel (Dry), page 154, using 3½ lb. honey. When the gravity drops to 5, feed with honey as for Mead (Sweet), page 151.

ORANGE MELOMEL (Sweet)

20 oranges
1 gal. (4·5 l.) water, approx.
1 tsp. pectolase
1 Campden tablet or 1 fl. oz. sulphite solution A
4–5 lb. (1·8–2·3 kg.) light honey
½ oz. (15 g.) citric acid
1 level tsp. grape tannin
1 level tsp. yeast nutrient
Tokay or all purpose yeast

Make as for Orange Melomel (Dry), page 154, using 3 lb. honey. When the gravity drops to 5, feed with honey as for Mead (Sweet), page 151.

Index